MASTERING GRAMMAR
BOOK ONE

Jo Kaufmann

CAMBRIDGE
THE ADULT EDUCATION COMPANY
New York • Toronto

Cambridge gratefully acknowledges the advice and contributions of the following adult educators who reviewed the draft version of this book:

Susan Adamowski, Assistant Dean, School of Continuing Education, Triton Community College, River Grove, Illinois

Marion E. Myers, Assistant Director of Programs for the Military—Atlantic Division, City Colleges of Chicago, Norfolk, Virginia

Stephen J. Steurer, Correctional Programs Specialist, National Institute for Corrections, Washington, D.C.

EXECUTIVE EDITOR: Brian Schenk
PRODUCTION MANAGER: Arthur Michalez
MANAGING EDITOR: Eileen Guerrin

Cover Design by Richard Shen

ISBN 0-8428-0175-8

9 8 7 6 5 4 3 2

FOREWORD

Most people think of grammar in much the same way they think of the flu: as something useless and unpleasant to which they were subjected at some time in their life. They were expected to learn countless grammatical terms for no particular purpose. Nothing was ever built on that terminology, so most of it was soon forgotten. They had dozens of do's and don't's thrust upon them, most of them unconnected and unexplained. From this ordeal, the vast majority emerged without real insights into the workings of the English language, and without much love or regard for the language.

Our businesses and colleges have long been complaining loudly that most of their new recruits do not know how to write good English. This has been blamed on the teachers, the students, and even the breakfasts the students eat; but it has never been blamed on the grammar books, which are for the most part remarkably similar and remarkably ineffective. Very few people will write good English unless they have some awareness of how the language functions. It is this awareness, as well as an interest in the English language, the students or readers will gain from this book.

This book covers the traditional categories of instruction: parts of speech, sentence parts, sentence types, correct usage, apostrophized words, and capitalization. What is frequently not traditional here is the organization and treatment of topics.

In most grammar books, any one topic—however multifaceted it may be—is covered in one prolonged bout and then never mentioned again. This may seem logical, and it does look neat in the table of contents, but memory research and the poor performance of our high school graduates have proved that this approach does not result in effective learning.

It is not only boring for students to plough endlessly through one topic: it is also a waste of everyone's time. Prescriptions and concepts that students cannot integrate into their own frame of reference do not sink in. Often, the requisite framework does not exist, since subsequent topics are needed to build it, and then the instruction is like water running off a duck's back. To prevent such waste of everyone's time and effort, this book presents the relatively complex topics—verbs, pronouns, subject-verb agreement—in several stages, places, and contexts. As students acquire a wider frame of reference, this type of instruction progresses in an ascending spiral, with repetition followed by new material.

This book gives many more reasons and explanations than other grammar books, whose unexplained do's and don't's are easy to formulate but hard to remember. The few explanations the standard grammar books do provide are hallowed by tradition, of course, but are often more mystifying than enlightening. "A sentence expresses a complete thought" will not reveal the nature of a sentence to anyone who had no clear conception of it beforehand. Such nebulous pronouncements will not be found here. The explanations offered in this book are not for the initiate, who does not need them, and many of them cover new ground.

The text is short but uncommonly full of examples. Wherever practical, an item of instruction is quickly followed by a practice exercise. In all, there are fifty-one exercise sections within the first five chapters, the teaching chapters. Chapter 6 will provide ready reference lists of irregular nouns and verbs. A special seventh chapter contains seven mastery tests. The first test in Chapter 7, labeled "Pretest," covers the full range of grammar skills and can be used to assess which parts of this book you should study most carefully. This test is followed by five chapter review tests, one for each of the core teaching chapters. These provide additional review activities for use after you've studied a chapter. The final test, labeled "Posttest," again covers the whole range of grammar skills and enables you to evaluate how much you've learned from your studies.

All this is not as forbidding as it may sound. Some of the exercises will raise a smile or a laugh. There is no need for grammar to be boring. It can be fascinating and enjoyable.

Contents

1. PARTS OF SPEECH

Every word in the language has two major properties: it carries certain limited meanings, and it also belongs to a class of words that functions in certain limited ways. The different word classes are the different parts of speech. What we will examine in this first section are the main members of each class, and how each class can function. We will divide the English language into nine word classes: nouns, verbs, adjectives, determiners, adverbs, pronouns, prepositions, conjunctions, and interjections.

NOUNS

Nouns identify all the concrete things we can touch, see, hear, smell, or taste.

> house   landscape   music   skunks   bitterness

Nouns also identify all our abstract concepts: things that are perceived by our mind, not by our senses.

> months   happiness   humor   biology

Common and Proper Nouns

Common nouns indicate what sort of people or things we are referring to.

> artist   children   cars

Proper nouns are the actual names by which particular people or things are known.

> Abraham Lincoln   Debbie   Mexico   Chevrolets

Common nouns are capitalized only at the beginning of a sentence. Proper nouns are capitalized at all times. (In Section 5, capitalization is discussed in detail.)

1

Can This Word Be a Common Noun?

To test whether a word can be used as a common noun, insert it into the following sentence.

The _____ pleased me.

If the sentence makes sense, the word can be used as a noun.

Singular and Plural

Nouns must be in one of two forms: the singular or the plural. The singular indicates one single thing. The plural indicates two or more things.

ONE:	dog	carrot	policy	hostess	man
TWO:	dogs	carrots	policies	hostesses	men

With most nouns, the plural is formed by adding -s to the end of the singular form.

ideas   trays   elephants   houses   shoes

With nouns whose singular form ends in s, sh, ch, x, or z, the plural is formed by adding -es to the singular form.

glasses   buses   bushes   churches   foxes   quizzes

With nouns that end in a consonant followed by -y, the y changes to i before -es is added.

city—cities   butterfly—butterflies

Note that nouns ending in a vowel followed by -y just add an s in the plural: boys, plays, holidays.

EXERCISE 1: In each sentence, underline the nouns, count them, and write in the answer blank how many nouns you found.

_____   1. Paul and Helen own a dog.

_____   2. My brother and sister own seven dogs.

_____   3. Could you tell me a story?

_____   4. He assured her that he loved her very much.

_____ 5. Costumes and scenery for this play were designed by Smith.

_____ 6. Bob, put your hat and gloves on the bench in the hall.

_____ 7. I looked for them but did not find them.

_____ 8. Sardinia is a small island off the coast of Italy.

EXERCISE 2: Capitalization and plural spellings are terrible here. Each sentence has two noun errors. Rewrite both noun forms correctly in the answer blank.

1. This Elevator will not be in Service today.

   _____

2. Bees and flys were hovering over our lunchs.

   _____

3. The employees and their familys had two picnics in the Park.

   _____

4. Daisies grew in the streets and alleies of this City.

   _____

5. Life has no certaintys other than death and taxs.

   _____

6. She spent the Holidays with her folks in michigan.

   _____

7. My Wife and I took three busses to get here.

   _____

8. The two companys in Chicago have entirely different Policies.

   _____

VERBS

We can put a great number of words together without making any real statement.

This old man at least seven cars

We have two perfectly good phrases here: *This old man,* and *at least seven cars.* But since we have no verb between the two phrases, we have no idea what connects the old man with the seven cars.

Action Verbs

Action verbs indicate what kind of an action someone or something performed, and when. They show whether the old man *owns, wants, considered, has ruined, had designed, will photograph,* or *will have sold* seven cars.

Nearly all verbs in the English language are action verbs, but we also use three other kinds of verbs: linking verbs, helping verbs, and modals.

Linking Verbs

Linking verbs don't show any action. They only connect someone or something with whatever this person or thing might *be* or *seem* like to us at some particular time.

> Puffins *are* birds.
> That speech *seemed* endless.
> This cake *will be* our contribution.
> The horn section *sounds* awful.
> The mattress *was* lumpy.
> Your outfit *will look* quite elegant.

The following verbs, in all their forms, can function as linking verbs.

look	feel	grow
smell	seem	become
taste	appear	remain
sound		stay

When we say, "This stew *looks, smells,* or *tastes* good," it is not the stew that has taken a peek or a whiff or a mouthful. *Stew* is the subject of the sentence, but the subject performs no particular action. It's the subject because we want to describe it.

The pillow *feels* soft.
Some criticism *appeared* necessary.
The pauses in their conversation *grew* longer.
My debts *became* a nightmare.
The hall *remained* empty.
This closet *will stay* a mess.

We may use some of those listed linking verbs quite often, but there is one linking verb we use all the time: the verb *to be* in all its forms.

George *was* the king of England.
You *will be* homecoming queen.
The dog *has been* an incredible pest.
The party *had been* successful, long, and expensive.
I *am* beautiful, clever, and modest.

Helping Verbs

Which verbs are helping verbs?
   They are the verbs *to be* and *to have* in all their various forms.
Whom do the helping verbs help?
   They help action verbs. They help linking verbs. They also help one another.
What kind of help do helping verbs provide?
   They help the other verbs to form most of their tenses.
What does *tense* mean?
   It means the verb form that shows whether an action *has been, is,* or *will be* performed. It means the verb form that shows whether something *has been, is,* or *will be* delightful.
What does *simple tense* mean?
   It is a verb tense you can form without the aid of a helping verb.
How many simple tenses are there?
   There are only two: the simple present and the simple past.

Simple Present	*Simple Past*
I drink	I drank
You seem	You seemed
It sits	It sat
They paint	They painted

All other tenses can only be formed with the help of *to be,* or *to have,* or both.

Modals

A modal does not show any action. A modal does not link. A modal cannot change its form. So what can a modal do?

A modal affects the meaning of the verb that follows it. All the following words are modals.

can	may
could	might
would	must
should	

Through the addition of different modals, you can give very different messages, even when the action word is the same.

you sing	I have gone
you can sing	I could have gone
you might sing	I would have gone
you should sing	I may have gone
	I must have gone

THE PRINCIPAL PARTS OF VERBS

Every verb has three basic forms, and these are known as its principal parts. The verbs *give, take, eat,* and *decide* will be our examples for showing the principal parts and the grammatical forms in which they occur.

The meaning and application of the various verb forms will be discussed under the heading "Verb Tenses, Voices, and Moods" in Section 4 (pages 69–75).

First Principal Part—The Plain Form

give	eat
take	decide

● The simple present uses the plain form.

I give	we eat
you take	they decide

In the simple present, the third person singular (he, she, it) must add -*s* or -*es* to the plain form.

he gives	it eats
she takes	the horse decides

- Questions formed with *do, does,* or *did* use the plain form.

                     did you give   did he eat
                     does it take   did the horse decide

- Negative statements formed with *do, does,* or *did* use the plain form.

                     I do not give   he did not eat
                     she does not take   they did not decide

- Statements with *do, does,* or *did* for emphasis use the plain form.

                  they did give it back   I do eat spinach
                  he does take milk   she did decide against it

- Modals can be used with the plain form.

                  we can give   she should eat
                  you must take   the horse might decide

- The future tense uses the plain form preceded by *will* or *shall*.

                  I will/shall give   the horse will eat
                  she will take   they will decide

- The infinitive uses the plain form preceded by *to*.

                     to give   to eat
                     to take   to decide

The infinitive is frequently used to identify a particular verb, as it is in the following sentence.

                  What are the principal parts of *to give*?

The infinitive follows a preceding action or linking verb.

(SIMPLE PRESENT)	I want to give he wants to take it seems to take
(SIMPLE PAST)	she wanted to eat they wanted to decide you appeared to decide
(FUTURE)	I shall/will want to give the horse will want to take
(PRESENT PERFECT)	he has wanted to eat you have wanted to decide
(PAST PERFECT)	she had wanted to give they had wanted to take

- The present participle uses the plain form with an -*ing* ending.

giving   eating

taking   deciding

If the plain form ends in -*e*, the *e* is eliminated when -*ing* is added.

give—givéing   take—takéing   decide—decidéing

What happens when -*ing* is added to verbs like *bat, slip, brag, stir, run,* or *forget*?

batting   slipping   bragging

stirring   running   forgetting

What is the rule for doubling the consonant before -*ing*?

If the plain form of the verb has only one syllable, and if that syllable ends in consonant–vowel–consonant, you double the last consonant.

skip—skipping

Some verbs whose plain form has two syllables also double their end consonant. Those that do are verbs like *control* and *forget*. They all have their accent on their last syllable, and their last syllable ends in consonant–vowel–consonant.

forget—forgetting

control—controlling

regret—regretting

Do not double the final consonant if the word does not follow the consonant—vowel—consonant pattern and does not have the accent on the last syllable.

reveal—revealing   travel—traveling

A *w* at the end of a syllable does not sound like a consonant and does not count as a consonant, so it is never doubled.

grow—growing

EXERCISE 3: For each plain form, list the verb's present participle (the -*ing* form) and try to spell it correctly.

1. take _____

2. review _____

3. sail _____

4. fret _____

5. grab _____

6. affect _____

7.	slink	_____	8.	entrap	_____
9.	flap	_____	10.	hover	_____
11.	drag	_____	12.	divide	_____
13.	draw	_____	14.	alarm	_____
15.	forbid	_____	16.	float	_____
17.	desire	_____	18.	bemoan	_____
19.	grip	_____	20.	console	_____

Note that the *-ing* form of many verbs can also be used as a noun.

> We studied accounting. Smoking is not permitted.
> I must do the ironing. Swimming is fun.

Second Principal Part—The Simple Past

> gave ate
> took decided

Our four verbs formed their past tense in different ways. *Give, take,* and *eat* changed their vowels. *Decide* merely added a *d* to its plain form.

All so-called regular verbs form the simple past by adding *-d* or *-ed* to their plain form. Verbs that use any other way of forming the simple past are known as irregular verbs.

A great number of verbs that consist of a single syllable, and some that consist of two syllables, are irregular verbs. That means, you can't guess what their second and third principal parts are. You have to know it or look it up. You can find quite a few of them on pages 112–115 of this book.

Third Principal Part—The Past Participle

> given eaten
> taken decided

Our four verbs formed their past participles in different ways. *Give* and *take* added *-n. Eat* added *-en. Decide* added *-d.*

All so-called regular verbs form their past participle by adding *-d* or *-ed.* Verbs that use any other way of forming their past participle are known as irregular verbs.

- The past participle is used to form the following tenses.

(PRESENT PERFECT)	I have given the horse has taken
(PAST PERFECT)	they had eaten she had decided
(FUTURE PERFECT)	you will have given we will have taken

- The past participle is used for all so-called passive forms of the verb.

(SIMPLE PRESENT)	I am given he is taken
(SIMPLE PAST)	they were eaten it was decided
(PRESENT PERFECT)	we have been given she has been taken
(PAST PERFECT)	they had been eaten it had been decided
(FUTURE PERFECT)	the horse will have been taken you will have been given

- The past participle is one of the verb forms that can be used with modals.

we could have given	you would be eaten
he might have taken	it should be decided

Some people make the mistake of using modals with the simple past. Modals can be used with the first principal part, the plain form. Modals can be used with the third principal part, the past participle. Modals can not be used with the second principal part, the simple past.

(WRONG)	we could have gave
(WRONG)	he might have took
(WRONG)	you would be ate

Why was there no example to show that the simple past of *decide* must not be used with a modal?

The simple past of *decide* is *decided*.
The past participle of *decide* is *decided*.

The second and third principal parts of *decide* have the same form. The second and third principal parts of every so-called regular verb have the same form.

> **The Principal Parts of** *GIVE, TAKE, EAT, DECIDE*
>
> *(1) Plain Form   (2) Simple Past   (3) Past Participle*
>
> | | | |
> |---|---|---|
> | give | gave | given |
> | take | took | taken |
> | eat | ate | eaten |
> | decide | decided | decided |

Regular Verbs and Irregular Verbs

Here are the principal parts of some regular verbs.

(1) Plain Form   (2) Simple Past   (3) Past Participle

talk	talked	talked
joke	joked	joked
remain	remained	remained
design	designed	designed
elevate	elevated	elevated

Regular verbs make the simple past and the past participle by adding *-d* or *-ed* to the plain form.

Here are the principal parts of some irregular verbs.

(1) Plain Form   (2) Simple Past   (3) Past Participle

go	went	gone
fly	flew	flown
bring	brought	brought
think	thought	thought
drink	drank	drunk
put	put	put
cost	cost	cost
break	broke	broken
sleep	slept	slept
begin	began	begun
drive	drove	driven

The only thing all irregular verbs have in common is that they don't use *-d* or *-ed* to form the simple past and the past participle. Therefore it is a mistake to put a *-d* or *-ed* ending onto an irregular verb.

(WRONG)   flied
(WRONG)   costed
(WRONG)   drived

It is also a mistake to use the second principal part (simple past) in constructions that must be formed with the third principal part (the past participle).

(WRONG)	we had went
(RIGHT)	we had gone
(WRONG)	they have broke
(RIGHT)	they have broken
(WRONG)	I was drove
(RIGHT)	I was driven

With irregular verbs, you have to know their principal parts; you can't guess them. If you don't know them for sure, or don't know whether a verb is regular or irregular, use the dictionary. Look up the plain form of the verb you're not sure about. If the verb is irregular, its other principal parts will be listed. If the verb turns out to be regular, its other principal parts will not be listed; so you know its other principal parts are both formed either with -d or with -ed.

Suppose you wanted to find the principal parts of *drive* in the dictionary. *Drive* is a verb, but *drive* is also a noun. Therefore the dictionary will have at least two entries for *drive*: one for the noun followed by *n* (for noun), and one for the verb followed by *v* (for verb) or followed by *vi* or *vt* (for verb, intransitive or verb, transitive). Only the verb entry lists the principal parts of irregular verbs.

After a verb like *bring*, the dictionary will list only one principal part: *brought*. That means the simple past and the past participle have the same form, which is *brought*.

EXERCISE 4: In each sentence, use the appropriate form of the verb in parentheses. You can check the principal parts of these verbs on pages 112–115 of this book.

1. The dog has _____ under the bed.   (hide)

2. It had _____ the plumber.   (bite)

3. I should have _____ the dog up in the kitchen.   (shut)

4. The dog must have _____ him for a burglar.   (mistake)

5. The plumber has _____ he will sue us.   (swear)

6. He could not have _____ a worse moment.   (choose)

7. Everything seems to have _____ to pieces.   (fall)

8. Our car has _____ down.   (break)

9. Our roof has _____ to leak.   (begin)

10. Our boiler has _____ out of fuel. (run)
11. That's why our water pipes had _____ . (freeze)
12. Then they had _____ . (burst)
13. So I had _____ the plumber my key. (give)
14. Then the dog had _____ itself on the plumber. (throw)
15. What is the name of the verb forms you chose? _____

EXERCISE 5: Under each sentence, list its action verb (AV), its helping verb or helping verbs (HV), and any modal (M) it may have.

1. You should have gone home sooner.

   AV _____*gone*_____ HV _____*have*_____ M _____*should*_____

2. He has been taking photographs of you.

   AV _____*taking*_____ HV _____*has been*_____ M _____

3. My aunt will be leaving by train.

   AV _____ HV _____ M _____

4. My uncle, her husband, will meet her at the station.

   AV _____ HV _____ M _____

5. The cats are sleeping, as usual.

   AV _____ HV _____ M _____

6. Pat may understand this book better than I.

   AV _____ HV _____ M _____

7. Pat may have understood this book better than I.

   AV _____ HV _____ M _____

8. The house could be seen from afar.

   AV _____ HV _____ M _____

9. She might be writing a novel.

   AV _____ HV _____ M _____

10. They had planted three apple trees and an oak.

    AV _____ HV _____ M _____

11. This dog is treated like a king.

AV _____ HV _____ M _____

12. The dog was always treated better than their cat.

AV _____ HV _____ M _____

ADJECTIVES

The sentence below has two blanks. Any word that sounds right in **one** of these blanks can function as an adjective.

Our _____ thing is too _____.

Adjectives describe things or people. In other words, adjectives refer directly to nouns or pronouns. Adjectives do not describe the performing of an action. In other words, adjectives do not refer directly to action verbs.

> My uncle was *generous*.
> My *generous* uncle was *rich*.
> My *generous, rich* uncle is *dead*.

> Her paintings are *huge*.
> They are *huge* but *hideous*.
> Her *huge, hideous* paintings amused me greatly.

The adjectives *generous, rich,* and *dead* referred directly to the noun *uncle*. The adjectives *huge* and *hideous* referred directly to the noun *paintings* and to the pronoun *they*. *Greatly* did not refer to *paintings*. It referred to the action verb *amused*. *Greatly* is always an adverb and never an adjective.

Facts of Life for Adjectives: Where Did They Come From?

All adjectives of one syllable, and some that have more, might be described as adjectives by birth. You cannot take them apart and find some other word hidden there. Such adjectives include the following.

true	good	green	large
new	bad	purple	small
old	thick	pure	soft
hot	smooth	bright	loud

Some words became adjectives by marriage: by combining a noun with an adjective ending. These include the following.

salt + *y* — salty
friend + *ly* — friendly
child + *ish* — childish
power + *full* — powerful
wood + *en* — wooden

murder + *ous* — murderous
accident + *al* — accidental
fault + *less* — faultless
magnet + *ic* — magnetic

Some adjectives by marriage combine a verb with an adjective ending, as do the following.

act + *ive* — active
break + *able* — breakable
prefer + *able* — preferable
discuss + *ible* — discussible
permit + *ible* — permissible
reverse + *ible* — reversible

terrify + *ic* — terrific
specify + *ic* — specific
defy + *ant* — defiant
comply + *ant* — compliant
abhor + *ent* — abhorrent
study + *ous* — studious

Some words we use and think of as adjectives are the present participles or the past participles of verbs.

an amusing man
a disgusting smell
the following words
my aching tooth
a stunning performance
cheering news
demanding customers
puzzling questions

frozen vegetables
fried onions
cooked meals
mashed potatoes
stolen goods
forbidden pleasures
broken promises
ground beef

Can an Adjective Become a Noun?

Adjectives always describe some thing or person that is mentioned in the sentence.

Our gray carpet is too dark.
Our ____ thing is too ____.

Both *gray* and *dark* describe a thing, namely, *carpet*. But what about the following sentence?

Our gray is too dark.

That sentence has no noun or pronoun to be described by *gray* and *dark*. *Gray* has become the thing that is described by the adjective *dark*. In this sentence, *gray* is functioning as a noun and is a noun.

Let's look at some further examples of words functioning either as adjectives or as nouns.

(1) The road was *rough*, but the ride was *smooth*.
(2) We learned to take the *rough* with the *smooth*.

In (1), *rough* is an adjective that describes the noun *road*, and *smooth* is an adjective that describes the noun *ride*. In (2), there is no noun for *rough* or *smooth* to describe. Do they describe the pronoun *We?* No, it's not *we* who are *rough* or *smooth*. *The rough* and *the smooth* are two things we must learn to take. The words *rough* and *smooth* are nouns in this sentence because they function as nouns.

Our *young* waiter was *efficient*.   (adjectives)
We want to hire the *young* and *efficient*.   (nouns)

The *good* fairy saved them from the *evil* dragon.   (adjectives)
Good triumphed over *evil*.   (nouns)

EXERCISE 6: In each sentence, indicate whether the word in italics is functioning as an adjective (A) or as a noun (N).

_____ **1.** The mosquitoes are *active* tonight.

_____ **2.** The *rich* fly first class.

_____ **3.** Saint Francis gave all his money to the *poor*.

_____ **4.** She left all her money to her *poor* relatives.

_____ **5.** Minnie is afraid of the *dark*.

_____ **6.** It was too *dark* to take photographs.

_____ **7.** The *blind* rely on their guide dogs.

_____ **8.** Traffic lights give no signals to the *blind*.

_____ **9.** They played music by *living* composers.

_____ **10.** He wrote for the *living*, not for posterity.

Can a Noun Become an Adjective?

Any word that sounds right in one of the blank spaces below can function an an adjective.

My _____ things   are too _____.

My floor   lamps   are too tall.
My sofa   cushions   are too soft.

My tea   cups   are too chipped.
My metal   shelves   are too dusty.
My ball   players   are too modest.

Most of the time, *floor, sofa, tea, metal,* and *ball* are used as nouns. Here they were used as adjectives that described *lamps, cushions, cups, shelves,* and *players.* If you put two nouns together, the first one becomes an adjective that describes the second one.

Can we prove that a noun preceding another noun becomes an adjective? Yes, we can. Nouns form a plural when they refer to more than one. Adjectives never form a plural.

one green apple
two hundred green apples

Apple changed to *apples* in the plural. *Green* remained *green,* though the noun it describes went into the plural.

In our sentences here, *lamps, cushions, cups, shelves, players,* are nouns or things in the plural. *Floor, sofa, tea, metal,* and *ball* are not in the plural. They behave like *green* or any other adjective here. Adjectives don't form a plural, even when the nouns they describe are in the plural.

DETERMINERS

The most common determiners are the articles: *an, a,* and *the.* A determiner relates directly to a noun. In fact, a determiner informs you that some word which could be a noun, a verb, or an adjective is now functioning as a noun.

you can *turn* (verb)   we *fine* you (verb)
the *turn* of events (noun)   made of *fine* wool (adjective)
a slow *turn* (noun)   paid a *fine* (noun)

Adjectives also relate directly to nouns. What is the difference between an adjective like *huge, nasty, pink, old,* and a determiner like *the* or *our?*

huge houses   houses were huge
the houses   houses were the

Determiners can only be used before the noun they relate to. Adjectives can be used before or after the noun they relate to. Furthermore, look at the order in which determiners and adjectives are used.

paid a fine   saw our house
paid a huge fine   saw our pink house
paid a huge, nasty fine   saw our pink, old house
paid a nasty, huge fine   saw our old, pink house

You can use adjectives in any order you like—*huge, nasty* or *nasty, huge*—and if you use a string of five adjectives, their order is up to you. But if you have a determiner as well as one or more adjectives, the determiner always comes first. It would sound very strange indeed to put the determiner anywhere else.

> paid nasty, huge a fine   saw pink, old our house

Articles

We use the articles *a, an,* and *the* all the time. When should we use *an,* and when should we use *a?*

We should use *an* when the next word begins with a vowel sound.

an apple	an owl
an elephant	an hour
an incredible din	an awful lot
an island	an oozing wound
an ox	an umpire
an honest man	an undertow

We should use *a* when the next word begins with a consonant sound.

a boat	a yard
a cook	a year
a historian	a user
a horse	a unit
a wonder	a European
a one-syllable word	a eulogy
a once-over	a eucalyptus tree

The word *the* is pronounced in two different ways: with a short vowel sound, and with a long one (as in *tree*). The use of long or short vowel sound corresponds exactly to the use of *an* or *a*. Use the long *e* sound (or *an*) before a word that begins with a vowel sound. Use the short vowel sound (or *a*) before a word that begins with a consonant sound.

Other Determiners

Words you can substitute for *the* can act as determiners.

the/this orange	the/that mouse
the/these oranges	the/those mice
the/our oranges	the/your mice

the/two oranges   the/forty mice
the/some oranges   the/few mice
the/all oranges   the/every mouse

EXERCISE 7: Write *an* or *a* before these words.

1. _____ hippopotamus   2. _____ iguana

3. _____ anteater   4. _____ unicorn

5. _____ spiny anteater   6. _____ hyena

7. _____ orangutan   8. _____ hedgehog

9. _____ hourglass spider   10. _____ ape

11. _____ ass   12. _____ kangaroo

13. _____ robin   14. _____ eagle

15. _____ European robin   16. _____ underdog

ADVERBS

We use an adverb to comment on the performing of an action: how, when, or where it is or was performed.

You pitch *well*.   She *always* whistled.
We played *badly*.   She *never* whistles.
They quarrel *abominably*.   She *often* whistles.
I agree *completely*.   She whistles *often*.
You drove *slowly*.   She *seldom* whistles.
It stops *suddenly*.   She whistled *here*.
He sang *magnificently*.   She whistled *there*.
She whistles *constantly*.   She whistled *everywhere*.
I searched *frantically*.   She whistled *nowhere*.

When you describe the how, when, or where of performing an action, it is wrong to use an adjective. You must use an adverb. Only an adverb describes an action verb.

(WRONG) He cooks good.   (WRONG) I dressed sloppy.
(RIGHT) He cooks well.   (RIGHT) I dressed sloppily.

(WRONG) She talks loud.   (WRONG) They behaved terrible.
(RIGHT) She talks loudly.   (RIGHT) They behaved terribly.

Luckily, most adjectives can be made into adverbs.

Turning Adjectives into Adverbs

Most often, you can just add -ly to the adjective, and there you have your adverb.

bad — badly	accidental — accidentally
great — greatly	faultless — faultlessly
serious — seriously	active — actively
childish — childishly	defiant — defiantly
powerful — powerfully	musical — musically
murderous — murderously	special — specially

With adjectives ending in consonant plus le, kill the e, and just add a y.

simple — simply	abominable — abominably
humble — humbly	believable — believably
subtle — subtly	horrible — horribly

With adjectives ending in consonant plus y, change the y to i, and then add -ly.

noisy — noisily	heavy — heavily
busy — busily	greedy — greedily
merry — merrily	funny — funnily
hazy — hazily	hasty — hastily

With adjectives ending in -ic, you add -ally to make them into adverbs.

specific — specifically	heroic — heroically
basic — basically	sarcastic — sarcastically
terrific — terrifically	frantic — frantically
horrific — horrifically	fantastic — fantastically
telepathic — telepathically	melodic — melodically

EXERCISE 8: Choose the adverb form to describe how something is or was performed. Choose the adjective form after a linking verb, which allows us to say what the subject is, was, or seemed like to us.

1. The lions were (hungry/hungrily) _____.

2. Our watchdog sleeps (sound/soundly) _____.

3. Emma sings (dreadful/dreadfully) _____.

4. This soup tastes (wonderful/wonderfully) _____.

5. His left ankle hurts (bad/badly) _____.

6. The exams were (murderous/murderously) _____.

7. That performance sounded (faultless/faultlessly) _____.

8. That performance went (faultless/faultlessly) _____.

We also use an adverb together with an adjective. Mostly that shows how seriously the adjective should be taken: to what extent or degree the adjective applies to something.

fairly late	*very* funny
totally stupid	*almost* believable
simply awful	*rather* hasty
really heavy	*so* beautiful
frequently busy	*too* big
greatly exaggerated	*not* fair

Finally, we also use adverbs together with other adverbs.

very slowly	rather well
not greatly	so marvelously
really badly	too slowly

PRONOUNS

Pronouns can take the place of nouns. We use pronouns because it gets boring to repeat or hear the same noun over and over again.

Once we have said "the American Revolution," we can use the pronoun *it* when we refer to the revolution for the second time in the same sentence. We could also use the pronoun *it* in the next sentence, provided it is quite clear that we mean *the American Revolution*. Suppose, though, that we had mentioned something like *England* in between, then *it* would refer to *England*. A pronoun always refers to the nearest preceding noun it agrees with.

Suppose we first mention *the American Revolution* and then *King George*. Now what would *it* refer to? *It* refers to *the American Revolution* because we never use *it* to refer to a person. The only pronouns that could agree with *King George* are *he, him, his, himself, who,* and *whom*.

The noun to which a pronoun refers is called its *antecedent*. If the noun is in the singular, then the pronoun that refers to it must also be in the singular. If the noun is in the plural, then the pronoun that refers to it must also be in the plural.

ONE MOUSE:	*it* nibbled	we heard *it*	*its* tail
	fed *itself*	the mouse *which/that* we heard	
TEN MICE:	*they* nibbled	we heard *them*	*their* tails
	fed *themselves*	the mice *which/that* we heard	

In the singular, most pronouns are sexist. They announce whether their antecedent is *masculine* (male), *feminine* (female), or *neuter* (a thing, or an animal whose sex is of no importance to us).

Personal Pronouns

We distinguish between singular and plural, and also between first person (the speaker), second person (the listener), and third person (another person or thing).

	SINGULAR		PLURAL	
FIRST PERSON	I	me	we	us
SECOND PERSON	you	you	you	you
THIRD PERSON	he she it	him her it	they	them

The first column under SINGULAR and PLURAL shows the form we use when the pronoun is the subject.

I ran   *they* stayed

The second column under SINGULAR and PLURAL shows the form we use when the pronoun is the object.

tigers chased *me*   lions ate *them*

Possessive Pronouns

Possessive pronouns show whose possessions we are talking about: whether something belongs to the speaker, the listener, to another person or thing, to several people including the speaker, to several listeners, or to some other people or things.

Most possessive pronouns have two forms. There is one form that is used together with a noun.

my shoe   *her* socks

The other form is used when the possessive pronoun stands by itself.

the shoe is *mine*   the socks are *hers*

	SINGULAR		PLURAL	
FIRST PERSON	my	mine	our	ours
SECOND PERSON	your	yours	your	yours
THIRD PERSON	his her its	his hers	their	theirs

Why is there no second form for *its?* Because you wouldn't say *That toy is its*. You would say something like *That toy is the cat's*.

Reflexive Pronouns

A reflexive pronoun refers to a noun or pronoun already in the sentence. It refers to the same person(s) or thing(s) as its antecedent.

the motor turns *itself* off   you served *yourselves*
they paid for it *themselves*   he *himself* said so

The rule for reflexive pronouns is very strict. You must always use a reflexive pronoun after an antecedent. You must never use a reflexive pronoun without an antecedent.

	SINGULAR	PLURAL
FIRST PERSON	myself	ourselves
SECOND PERSON	yourself	yourselves
THIRD PERSON	himself herself itself	themselves

EXERCISE 9: Write the correct pronoun in each answer blank.

1. He gave the key to (me/myself) _____.

2. (Herself/She) _____ had taken the key.

3. Dan and (myself/I) _____ took the bus.

4. We recognized (ourselves/us) _____ in the photo.

5. We recognized (yourselves/you) _____ in the photo.

6. Any cat washes (themselves/itself) _____.

7. I tried to find (me/myself) _____ a good seat.

8. We have already introduced (ourself/ourselves) _____

Demonstrative Pronouns

You know that the words *this, that, these,* and *those* can be determiners taking the place of *the* before a noun. The words *this, that, these,* and *those* can also be used on their own instead of a noun.

> I would like some of this.
> That is not enough.
> These look fresher than those.

When they do not precede a noun, *this, that, these,* and *those* are said to be demonstrative pronouns. They are pronouns because they take the place of nouns. They are called demonstrative because that means "used for pointing out." All they do is point to something without naming it; so to use demonstrative pronouns can be a rather inexact way of expressing yourself.

This and *that* refer to nouns in the singular. *These* and *those* refer to nouns in the plural.

> (WRONG) This is enough carrots.
> (RIGHT) These are enough carrots.

> (WRONG) That are some of the things I wanted to mention.
> (RIGHT) Those are some of the things I wanted to mention.

Relative Pronouns

Let's take three sentences. The first one is our original statement. The second and third are explanations we want to add to our original statement.

(1) The actor gets $200 a week.
(2) The actor plays the lead.
(3) $200 a week is not enough.

We could combine the three sentences by using the relative pronouns *who* and *which*.

The actor who plays the lead gets $200 a week,
which is not enough.

A relative pronoun is like a two-way plug. It allows you to connect a word or phrase in the sentence with an explanation of that word or phrase. *Who* connected *the actor* to an explanation. *Which* connected *$200 a week* to an explanation. To introduce such explanations into a sentence, we use the following relative pronouns.

who   whom   whose   which   that

To introduce explanations about people, we use *who, whom, whose*.
To introduce explanations about things, we use *that* or *which*.

the dancer *who* performed last night
the dancer *whom* I saw yesterday
the dancer *whose* partner fell on the floor
the dance *that* was performed yesterday
the dance, *which* is too long, was performed

When adding explanations about things (as in the last two examples above), some people use *which* only for an explanation that could be left out and is put between commas. When the explanation cannot be left out and is not put between commas, they insist that the relative pronoun must be *that* and not *which*.

Note that it is wrong to use *what* as a relative pronoun.

(WRONG)   the book what you lent me
(RIGHT)   the book that you lent me
(RIGHT)   the book which you lent me

Indefinite Pronouns

everybody	somebody	anybody	nobody
everyone	someone	anyone	no one
everything	something	anything	nothing

All the above are indefinite pronouns. What is indefinite is the identity of the person or thing they represent. One thing is definite though: each of these pronouns represents only one person or thing (or a group spoken of as one single group). Therefore, when one of these indefinite pronouns is the subject of a sentence, its verb must be in the singular. One look at the pronouns themselves will show you why. Each one is a combination of *every, some, any,* or *no* with the singulars *body, one,* or *thing.*

everybody knows	does anybody know	nobody pays
everyone has seen	has anyone seen	nothing is lost

Some, Any, or No?

It depends on the rest of your sentence whether your indefinite pronouns should start with *some-*, or *any-*, or *no-*.

(1) I saw somebody, someone, something.
(2) Did you see anybody, anyone, anything?
(3) I did not see anybody, anyone, anything.
(4) I saw nobody, no one, nothing.

Here are the rules which govern these four sentences.

(1) Pronouns with *some-* are used for positive statements.
(2) Pronouns with *any-* are used in questions.
(3) Pronouns with *any-* are used when the verb is accompanied by a negative, such as *not, never, hardly, scarcely.*
(4) Pronouns with *no-* are used when the verb is not accompanied by a negative *(not, never, without, hardly, scarcely).*

Note that sentences (3) and (4) are negative statements. Both mean the same thing but express it in different ways. You can choose one way or the other, but don't use both in the same sentence.

(WRONG)	I never saw nobody.
(RIGHT)	I never saw anybody.
(RIGHT)	I saw nobody.

(WRONG)   She doesn't know nothing.
(RIGHT)   She doesn't know anything.
(RIGHT)   She knows nothing.

If you want to make a negative statement, it is illogical to use two negatives, as the following will prove.

he is not dead = he is alive
he is not not dead = he is dead
he is never not dead = he is dead

For the same reason you must not add a negative to *without, hardly,* or *scarcely. Without, hardly,* and *scarcely* are negatives in themselves.

(WRONG)   We tried to build it without no nails.
(RIGHT)   We tried to build it without any nails.

(WRONG)   You cannot fix it without no hammer.
(RIGHT)   You cannot fix it without a hammer.

(WRONG)   He didn't hardly take anything.
(RIGHT)   He hardly took anything.

EXERCISE 10: In the following sentences the indefinite pronouns were left incomplete. Complete them correctly by adding either *some-* or *any-* or *no-*.

1. I haven't forgotten _____thing.

2. I would like you to meet _____one.

3. Can we believe _____body?

4. They will not be invited by _____one.

5. He is a loner and speaks to _____body.

6. He is a loner who doesn't speak to _____body.

7. She did it alone without _____one's help.

8. You have eaten hardly _____thing.

PREPOSITIONS

We can use prepositions to show how one thing or action relates to another in space, in time, or in our mind.

    Here is a sentence that needs a preposition, followed by the same sentence with various prepositions.

Your grandmother was sitting ——— the table.

Your grandmother was sitting at the table.
Your grandmother was sitting under the table.
Your grandmother was sitting on the table.

All the following words are prepositions.

about	by	over
above	concerning	past
across	despite	pending
after	down	regarding
against	during	respecting
along	except	since
amid	excepting	through
among	for	throughout
around	from	to
as	in	toward
at	inside	under
before	into	underneath
behind	like	until
below	of	unto
beneath	off	up
beside	on	upon
besides	onto	with
between	out	within
beyond	outside	without

There are also the following prepositions that consist of more than one word.

according to	in spite of
apart from	instead of
aside from	on account of
as to	on top of
because of	out of
	owing to

One mistake that is often made is to think that *off* should be followed by *of*. It should not.

(WRONG) I took the picture off of the wall.
(RIGHT) I took the picture off the wall.

A preposition affects the noun(s) or pronoun(s) following it.

into *the snowstorm*   behind *us*
because of *the rain*   to *her and him*
throughout *the world*   without *you or me*

The noun(s) or pronoun(s) following a preposition can never be the subject of a sentence. If a preposition precedes them, they must be objects. Therefore a pronoun or two pronouns after a preposition must always be in the object form.

EXERCISE 11: Choose the right pronoun form in each sentence.

1. There was no one present beside (I/me) _____.
2. Mary and (he/him) _____ were standing in the rain.
3. This package arrived for you and (he/him) _____.
4. You and (I/me) _____ have nothing in common.
5. He should buy a ticket from you or (they/them) _____.
6. Between you and (I/me) _____, I thought it was boring.
7. We will go instead of (they/them) _____.
8. This letter was drafted by Robert and (I/me) _____.

CONJUNCTIONS

The conjunction we use every two minutes is *and*. All conjunctions are connectors.

Conjunctions connect words.

bats *and* birds   over *or* under
flew *and* squeaked   you *or* me

Conjunctions connect phrases.

to have your cake *and* eat it, too
catching the fish *or* buying it
wearing socks *but* no shoes

Conjunctions connect clauses, which means: they convert two sentences into one.

> She bought the present, *and* I baked the cake.
> You eat that cake, *or* I'll box your ears.
> I tiptoed *because* you were resting.
> You tiptoed, *but* you sang very loudly.
> You made a great noise *although* I was resting.
> *Although* I was resting, you made a great noise.
> They sulked *after* I told them off.
> *After* I told them off, they sulked.

All the following words can be used as conjunctions.

after	before	unless	where
although	if	until	whereas
as	since	when	wherever
because	though	whenever	while

Conjunctions that do or can consist of more than one word include the following.

as far as	as though	provided (that)
as if	considering (that)	so (that)
as long as	in order that	supposing (that)

> You yelled *as if* you had been stung by a bee.
> They will sing *provided* you play the piano.
> *Supposing* we bought a kangaroo, where would we put it?

INTERJECTIONS

The first thing we say when we have dropped something, bumped into something, or received unexpected good news is most often an interjection. It's either some sound, or some word, or some phrase which shows our great surprise, great pleasure, or great displeasure. That is the only purpose or meaning of the sounds, words, or phrases we use on such occasions.

In writing, if such an interjection or exclamation stands by itself, it should be followed by an exclamation mark.

> Ouch!   Heavens!   Good grief!   Great Scott!

If the interjection is followed by a sentence, we use a comma to separate the emotional outburst from the real sentence.

> For Pete's sake, someone has stolen my bicycle!
> Heavens above, where are those keys?
> Wow, I never thought you could win that much!
> Oh, I think I have come to the end of the chapter.

For additional practice, turn to the review test for this chapter at the back of the book.

2. PARTS OF THE SENTENCE

The shortest sentence in English is: *Go!* That, as you know, is a command sentence, not the ordinary kind of sentence. What we will be investigating for a while now are the more ordinary sentences, namely, statement sentences. We will investigate their various parts, and how those parts relate to one another.

SUBJECT and VERB

The shortest statement sentence in English is: *I go.* It has a subject (*I*) and a verb (*go*), and that is the minimum of parts. Now suppose we substitute *he* for *I.* We would get: *He go.* Is that a correct sentence? You know that it isn't, but why isn't it? It isn't a correct sentence because the subject (*he*) does not agree with the verb (*go*). So the minimum we require in a sentence is three things:

   (1)   a subject
   (2)   a verb
   (3)   agreement between the subject and its verb

All we need to do now is to define what we mean by the *subject* and *verb* of a sentence, and by *agreement* between the two.

Subject

The subject of a sentence is the person(s) or thing(s) whose nature or actions the sentence discusses.

   (a)   *George* forgot to buy paint.
   (b)   *That* is a pity
   (c)   In our kitchen, the *ceiling and walls* were peeling.
   (d)   *We* have been scraping and plastering them.
   (e)   *Scraping and plastering* are more difficult than painting.
   (f)   To tell the truth, *everyone* hates scraping.
   (g)   The *color* we chose for our walls is green.
   (h)   Our kitchen *chairs* have green seats.
   (i)   *Green* is my favorite color.

As you can see, two types of words function as subjects: nouns and pronouns.

Number and Person

When the subject is a personal pronoun, you know whether it is first, second, or third person singular or plural. When the subject is a noun, you know whether it is plural or singular, but can you tell what person a noun subject is? You ask yourself which personal pronoun would replace the noun subject.

John sings = He sings

Mary sings = She sings

The bird sings = It sings

Whales sing = They sing

A noun in the singular is third person singular.

A noun in the plural is third person plural.

Now take a double subject, a so-called compound subject.

The dog and the whale sang.

There were two who sang (dog and whale), *they sang*. So this subject is in the third person plural.

Now take a compound subject consisting of two personal pronouns linked by *and*.

You and I sang.

Which single pronoun would you use to replace *You and I*? You would say, *We sang,* so this compound subject would be first person plural.

We can now analyze the subjects of our nine lettered sentences.

(a) a proper noun, third person singular
(b) a demonstrative pronoun, third person singular
(c) a compound subject, two nouns linked by *and,* third person plural
(d) a personal pronoun, subject form, first person plural
(e) a compound subject, two *-ing* forms functioning as nouns linked by *and,* third person plural
(f) an indefinite pronoun, third person singular
(g) a noun, third person singular
(h) a noun, third person plural
(i) an adjective functioning as a noun, third person singular

There are three things we want to know about the subject of a sentence.

(1) What is the simple subject of the sentence?
(2) Does the simple subject amount to a singular or a plural?
(3) Does the simple subject amount to first, second, or third person singular or plural?

Simple Subject—Complete Subject

The simple subject is the thing or things, person or persons, whose nature or actions the sentence discusses.

Larry   balloons   anatomy   we   the dog and I

The complete subject consists of the simple subject and whatever details or explanations are used to describe it.

Dear little Larry is out.
Larry, my next-door neighbor, is out.

Gigantic blue balloons rose into the sky.
My old great-uncle's favorite balloons rose into the sky.

The anatomy of dinosaurs and mammals interested me.
The anatomy I was taught in school interested me.

We, whose address nobody knows, are leaving.
We, who have eaten ourselves to a standstill, are leaving.

Clementine Robinson's dog and I were waiting.
A large, vicious dog and I were waiting.

Only the simple subject is of interest when you investigate the subject of a sentence. You disregard the descriptions and explanations that accompany the simple subject. Then you decide whether the subject of the sentence is first, second, or third person singular or plural.

Taking the simple subjects we have been using, you would decide as follows.

Larry: third person singular (like *he*)
balloons: third person plural (like *they*)
anatomy: third person singular (like *it*)
we: first person plural (like *the dog and I*)
the dog and I: first person plural (like *we*)

EXERCISE 12: In each sentence, find the simple subject. Copy it onto the answer line. Then state on the answer line whether the subject is singular or plural, and in the first, second, or third person.

1. The lady who wrote to us lives in Pittsburgh.

   _____

2. On Wednesday evening he will come for dinner.

   _____

3. The house in which I live is quite large.

   _____

4. The hands of the gorilla seemed remarkably human.

   _____

5. One pear and one apple remained in the dish.

   _____

6. Perhaps you and I could meet for dinner.

   _____

7. The sleeves of my old gray coat got ripped.

   _____

8. The parrot we saw talks very well.

   _____

Verb and Verb Phrase

Our minimum sentence consists of a subject and a verb. In the simple present and simple past, the verb consists of only one word.

> I go   I went   she goes   she went

In all other tenses, a main verb, such as *go*, also needs one or more helping verbs.

> I *am going*   she *is going*
>
> I *was going*   she *was going*
>
> I *will be going*   she *will be going*

I *have gone*	she *has gone*
I *have* not *gone*	she *has* not *gone*
I *had gone*	she *had gone*
I *will have gone*	she *will have gone*

This combination of a main verb and its helping verbs is called a verb phrase. A verb phrase may also include a modal, an infinitive, and *do, does, did.*

I *might be going*	she *might be going*
I *should have gone*	she *should have gone*
I *am going to give*	she *is going to give*
I *do* not *go*	she *does* not *go*

Do some detective work on these examples, and find the answer to this question: Which part of the verb phrase agrees with the subject?

Agreement of Subject and Verb

A verb or verb phrase has to agree with its subject in number and person.

NO AGREEMENT	AGREEMENT
I are	I am
you was	you were
we sits	we sit
I has seen	I have seen
she don't know	she doesn't know
he were sitting	he was sitting
you has left	you have left
the dog have gone	the dog has gone
the dogs has gone	the dogs have gone
the cat have been seen	the cat has been seen

Is it clear to you now which part of the verb phrase has to agree with the subject? It's the helping verb; and if there is more than one helping verb in the verb phrase, it's the first helping verb that has to agree with the subject. What else? *Do* and *does* or *don't* and *doesn't* must agree with the subject if they are the first part of the verb phrase.

EXERCISE 13: None of the following sentences is correct. They have no agreement between subject and verb or verb phrase. Correct each verb or verb phrase so that it agrees with the subject of the sentence.

1. The rabbits has nibbled _____ these cabbages.

2. The farmer don't know _____ there's a hole in his fence.

3. My brother and sister has seen _____ the hole.

4. They was passing _____ the fence yesterday.

5. The hole don't look _____ very big.

6. You needs to get _____ quite close before you see it.

EXERCISE 14: In each sentence, underline the simple subject. Then choose the verb form that agrees with the subject.

1. A bird with white wing tips (was/were) _____ sitting here.

2. The trees that you planted (has/have) _____ new leaves.

3. My husband and I (was/were) _____ hoping you would call.

4. Maybe the bulbs in this lamp (has/have) _____ burnt out.

5. The man to whom you introduced me (has/have) _____ been married seven times.

6. Because of the rain, the festivities in the park (was/were) _____ canceled.

7. Under these difficult circumstances, everybody (has/have) _____ been most helpful.

8. Despite a lot of requests, the program on training dogs and their owners (has/have) _____ not been shown on TV so far.

Subject and Compound Verb

The following sentences have what is called compound verbs.

> The whale sings and swims.
> The dog sings and barks.

A sentence with a compound verb has two verbs or verb phrases to show what the subject does, did, will do, is, was, or will be. Both verbs or verb phrases relate equally to the same subject, so both must agree with it.

> He *has been spoiled* and *is* a pest.
> I *have been spoiled* and *am* a pest.

If the helping verb(s) in both verb phrases would be the same, we do not usually repeat the helping verb(s). We use the helping verb(s) in the first verb phrase, but not in the second.

> She *has eaten* the cake and *(has) drunk* all the coffee.
> You *were sitting* at home and *(were) watching* TV.
> They *have been seen* and *(have been) heard*.
> They *have been seen* or *(have been) heard*.
> They *have been seen* but *(have)* not *(been) heard*.

DIRECT OBJECT

Someone or something (the subject) performs an action (verb), and this may directly involve someone or something else (the direct object).

> We ate.   We ate pie.
> Alex returned.   Alex returned the umbrella.
> They remembered.   They remembered him.
> You understand.   You understand us.
> Minnie spoke.   Minnie spoke Japanese.
> He chose.   He chose green.

The subject and verb come first, and then the direct object tells us what or whom the subject and verb affected.

> We ate what?   pie
> Alex returned what?   the umbrella
> They remembered whom?   him
> You understand whom?   us
> Minnie spoke what?   Japanese
> He chose what?   green

Direct objects are nouns, words that function as nouns, or pronouns. When pronouns are objects, they must, of course, be in their object form. Which pronoun objects did we use in our examples?

Let us now look at the verbs in our examples. All those verbs can be used either with or without a direct object. There are many verbs that can function in both ways. There are others that can function in one way only. Some make no sense with a direct object. Some make no sense without a direct object.

Intransitive Verbs

An intransitive verb is a verb that makes sense without a direct object. In the dictionary, such verbs are followed by the letters *vi*, meaning *verb, intransitive.*

Some intransitive verbs can never be used with a direct object. Why not? There are some things you can do, but you can't do them to someone or something else. Take the following verbs, for example.

sleep	lie	cough	belong
doze	fall	sneeze	rejoice
die	stumble	blush	glow

You can sleep, doze, or lie, but you can't sleep, doze, or lie some other person or thing. These verbs can only be intransitive, but verbs like *eat* can be used either intransitively (without a direct object) or transitively (with a direct object).

Transitive Verbs

A transitive verb is a verb that can be followed by a direct object. In the dictionary, such verbs are followed by the letters *vt*, meaning *verb, transitive.* Verbs that can be used either with or without a direct object are followed by *vi/vt* in the dictionary.

Some verbs are only transitive. They make no sense if they are not followed by a direct object. It's not a complete or sensible statement to say, *I keep, I give, I love,* unless we say whom or what I keep, give, and love.

Here are some further examples of verbs used only transitively (followed by a direct object).

buy	praise	find	accompany
borrow	insult	mail	adore
lend	annoy	beat	encourage

Modified and Compound Direct Objects

A direct object need not consist of only one noun or pronoun. We can add descriptions or explanations to it, just as we can add descriptions and explanations to a subject.

> You ate pie.
> You ate my pie.
> You ate apple pie.
> You ate that huge pie.
> You ate more pie than anyone else.
> You ate the pie I had baked.
> You ate the pie which I was going to serve tomorrow.

You can also use compound direct objects.

> You ate the whole pie and all the brownies.
> You ate pie, brownies, seven hot dogs, and some pickles.

No matter what description or explanation we attach, *pie* plus our description or explanation of it answers the question, *You ate what?* In exactly the same way, the compound direct object answers the question, *You ate what?*

Here are some compound direct objects that answer the question, *You like whom or what?*

> You like Fran, Brian, and me.
> You like Fran's cooking, Brian's, and mine.

In the first of these two sentences, what kind of a word is *me?* In what form is it? Why is it in that form? In the second of the two sentences, what kind of a word is *mine?* What does it refer to? Why is it in this form?

Position in the Sentence

Look at the following group of words, which has a subject, a verb phrase, and a direct object.

> Will persuade my cousin your sister.

You know that somebody will persuade. You know which two people are involved. Why can't you tell who will be persuading whom?

English requires a strict word order, more so than many other languages. In English, we often depend on the word order to tell us which noun is the subject, and which is the direct object. In almost every case, a statement sentence must have this word order:

Subject — Verb — Direct Object

Your sister will persuade my cousin.
My cousin will persuade your sister.

When you try to make a sentence clear and easy to understand, put subject, verb, direct object, as close together as you can.

OBJECT OF A PREPOSITION

A noun or a pronoun that follows a preposition is the object of that preposition. A pronoun as the object of a preposition must, of course, be in its object form.

at *night*   for *us*

The object of a preposition may consist of more than one noun or pronoun.

at *the stroke of midnight*   for *us and our children*

Together, a preposition and its object form a phrase that is known as a *prepositional phrase*. A prepositional phrase gives added meaning to a noun, to a pronoun, or to a verb in the sentence.

A child passed us.
A child *in a witch's costume* passed us.
She bought a coat.
She bought a coat *with a fur collar*.
Everyone owns a dog.
Everyone *in my building* owns a dog.
The telephone rang.
The telephone rang *at the stroke of midnight*.

As you know, some verbs cannot be followed by a direct object. But every verb can be followed by a preposition and the object of that preposition. To show that this is so, we'll use the intransitive verbs that were listed before.

I slept *like a log.*
They dozed *after the meal.*
He will die *of disappointment.*
You were lying *on the grass.*
Someone could fall *over these sticks.*
Everyone stumbled *in the dark.*
She coughed *into her handkerchief.*
They blushed *with embarrassment.*
Everything belongs *to us.*
We rejoiced *with them.*
Something was glowing *under the ashes.*

Position in the Sentence

A prepositional phrase that gives added meaning to either a noun or a pronoun should directly follow that noun or pronoun.

A prepositional phrase that gives added meaning to the verb can directly follow the verb in such sentences as you saw in the last set of examples. None of those sentences have a direct object. In sentences with a direct object, the verb's prepositional phrase cannot follow the verb directly. The direct object follows the verb, and the prepositional phrase follows the direct object.

We sang /hymns/ in church.
He told /lies/ without end.
You met /her/ for the second time.
I saw /you/ before him.
She phoned /my son/ instead of me.
They sent /a letter/ to her.

INDIRECT OBJECT

With certain verbs, we can use an indirect object instead of using a preposition and its object.

OBJECT OF PREPOSITION:	They sent /a letter/ *to her.*
INDIRECT OBJECT:	They sent *her* /a letter/.
OBJECT OF PREPOSITION:	We bought /a dress/ *for our daughter.*
INDIRECT OBJECT:	We bought *our daughter* /a dress/.

The verbs that can take an indirect object are verbs like *give, wish, send, cook, bake, make, bring, fetch, show,* and *tell.* They are the verbs we can use to describe what we do *for* somebody else or give *to* somebody else.

> You baked *Grandma* a cake.
> You baked a cake *for Grandma.*
> We gave *the dog* a bone.
> We gave a bone *to the dog.*

The only prepositional objects that can become indirect objects are those preceded by *to* or *for.*

Position in the Sentence

An indirect object can only be used in a sentence that has a direct object also. The indirect object is always placed between the verb and the direct object. In fact, aside from words modifying the direct object, an indirect object is the only thing that should ever be placed between the verb and the direct object.

If a sentence sounds awkward with an indirect object, don't use an indirect object. If your indirect object has lots of syllables, it may be better not to wedge it in between the verb and the direct object. Make your indirect object into the object of *to* or *for,* and place the whole thing after the direct object.

(AWKWARD)	She wished the president, his associates, and his helpers /every success/.
(BETTER)	She wished /every success/ to the president, his associates, and his helpers.
(AWKWARD)	He had bought the most wonderful woman in the world /a diamond ring/.
(BETTER)	He had bought /a diamond ring/ for the most wonderful woman in the world.
(AWKWARD)	They told their children, grandchildren, nephews, and nieces /everything/.
(BETTER)	They told /everything/ to their children, grandchildren, nephews, and nieces

SUBJECT COMPLEMENT

A noun or adjective that follows a linking verb is a subject complement.

Linking verbs don't have objects. Objects are involved in some action that is performed by the subject. The subject of a linking verb does nothing at all, and the linking verb has only one function: it allows us to pinpoint the subject or express our opinion of the subject.

> His nose seemed *immense*.
> The man's name was *Cyrano*.
> The man in the picture is *my uncle*.
> Your uncle looks *vicious*.

We can, of course, use several adjectives or nouns in the subject complement.

> The soup tasted *burnt and salty*.
> This car is a *wreck and a menace*.

We can add adverbs to the complement adjectives. We can add adjectives to the complement nouns.

> The music sounded *unusually hideous*.
> Your friend is *an incompetent painter*.
> Your friend is a *remarkably incompetent painter*.

You can also use pronouns as subject complements. Since a linking verb can't have an object, we don't use the object form of a personal pronoun. The subject form of the personal pronoun is used in the subject complement.

> The person who burned and salted the soup was *I*.
> The worst cooks we had were *you and she*.

EXERCISE 15: With each sentence, identify the word(s) in italics as either a direct object (DO), an indirect object (IO), the object of a preposition (OP), or a subject complement (SC).

_____ 1. We will bake *Nancy* a chocolate cake.

_____ 2. Brian was riding *a gray horse*.

_____ 3. He told her *the same joke* three times.

_____ 4. All the dresses we saw were *too expensive*.

_____ 5. The only person who could afford them is *Jacqueline*.

————— **6.** You can go without *me*.

————— **7.** There is not much point to *this story*.

————— **8.** The critics praised *that film* to the skies.

————— **9.** The cat was hiding behind *the door*.

————— **10.** We wish *you* a very happy birthday.

————— **11.** In his thirties, Napoleon became *Emperor of France*.

————— **12.** They have been telling *us* tremendous lies.

For additional practice, turn to the review test for this chapter at the back of the book.

3. SENTENCE TYPES

STATEMENTS—Declarative Sentences

All declarative sentences begin with a capital letter and end with a period. Is there a declarative sentence in the following dialogue?

"Where should I look for the keys?"
"In the table drawer or on my dresser."

The first line ends with a question mark, so it can't be declarative. The second line ends with a period, so is that a declarative sentence?

The second line is no sentence of any kind. It's merely the answer to a question, and it has practically no meaning if you don't know the question that preceded it. The most important feature of a sentence is that it is complete in itself and makes sense on its own.

The minimum and the core of a declarative sentence are its subject and verb. You know, however, that with some verbs more is needed. *"I am"* may be a good answer to *"Are you hungry?"* but it makes no sense on its own. So subject and verb are not enough when the verb is a linking verb. With a linking verb, the sentence core and the absolute minimum are: subject, linking verb, subject complement.

I am hungry.   I am Ron.   I am a student.

With action verbs, you can put an intransitive verb after a subject and get a complete sentence. You can do the same with a verb that can either be transitive or intransitive.

He sneezed.   She was driving.

With verbs that can only be transitive, it takes an object as well as a subject to make a declarative sentence. *"I buy"* may be a good answer to *"Do you buy or sell?"* but it is not a complete sentence. We expect an object after a verb that is always transitive.

I bought eggs.   You found the keys.
We adore cats.   They encouraged us.

We do not expect those four sentences to continue. It is the essence of a complete sentence that you do not expect it to continue.

Clauses

Strangely enough, you can make complete sentences incomplete by adding a word.

When I bought eggs   *Until* you found the keys
Although we adore cats   *Because* you encouraged us

We made these sentences begin with a conjunction, and now they can no longer stand on their own. Because they are preceded by a conjunction, they've lost their completeness and their independence. They have become dependent clauses. To make them into complete sentences, we have to add an independent clause to each.

When I bought eggs, I bought some for you.
Although we adore cats, our dog hates them.
Until you found the keys, we sheltered under a tree.
Because they encouraged us, we continued to practice.

The clauses used to complete these sentences are independent because they could stand on their own. The clauses that begin with a conjunction are dependent because they cannot stand on their own.

EXERCISE 16: Some of the following sentences are complete, and some are incomplete. Mark a complete sentence with a C in the answer blank. With an incomplete sentence, use the answer blank to state what the sentence needs. Use SC for subject complement. Use DO for direct object. Use IC for independent clause.

_____ 1. We did not believe her.

_____ 2. Unless we hear from you immediately.

_____ 3. The child, who was three years old, wanted.

_____ 4. For her birthday, we gave her.

_____ 5. The apple pie and the peach ice cream tasted.

_____ **6.** After a few years, George became.

_____ **7.** You tried to find your way in the dark.

_____ **8.** After we had left the house.

QUESTIONS—Interrogative Sentences

An interrogative sentence asks a direct question and must therefore end with a question mark. Interrogative sentences have a different word order from declarative sentences.

DECLARATIVE	INTERROGATIVE
They are polite.	Are they polite?
It is late.	Is it late?
You were there.	Were you there?
The car was a wreck.	Was the car a wreck?

In a declarative sentence, the subject precedes the verb. In an interrogative sentence, a verb precedes the subject.

The question sentence may have a verb phrase, not just a single verb. In that case, the first word of the verb phrase precedes the subject, and the rest of the verb phrase follows the subject.

DECLARATIVE	INTERROGATIVE
You *were sitting* down.	*Were* you *sitting* down?
We *should have gone.*	*Should* we *have gone?*
It *has been sold.*	*Has* it *been sold?*
They *would have tried to sell* it.	*Would* they *have tried to sell* it?

EXERCISE 17: Rewrite the following sentences in question form. Then state whether the first word of your question is a helping verb (HV) or a modal (M).

1. Bats can fly.

_____

2. Dogs must bark.

_____

3. Anne would have seen me.

_____

4. We should be sleeping now.

_____

5. You will have gone by then.

_____

6. They had been lost.

_____

7. The cat has been sleeping.

_____

8. The guests are beginning to leave.

_____

A question sentence can begin with a helping verb or a modal, but it cannot begin with an action verb. *You live here* cannot be turned into *Live you here?*

Action verbs form most of their tenses with helping verbs, so in most tenses, there is a helping verb that can precede the subject of a question sentence. Only the simple present and simple past of an action verb are formed without any helping verbs. So what will precede the subject then?

Do, Does, Did

For a question in the simple present, an action verb uses *do* or *does*, *don't* or *doesn't* to precede the subject.

Does or *doesn't* are used for the third person singular (*he, she, it,* or a noun in the singular). *Do* or *don't* are used for all other persons, singular or plural.

> Does Olga live here?
> Doesn't she live here?
> Do I ring this bell?
> Don't these bells work?

For a question in the simple past, an action verb uses *did* or *didn't* to precede the subject. All persons, singular or plural, use *did* or *didn't*.

> Did Shakespeare write plays?
> Didn't he write musical comedies?

Note that the plain form of the verb must be used with *did, didn't, do, don't, does, doesn't*. *Did* or *didn't* express the past tense, but the main verb should not. It is wrong to use anything but the plain form of the main verb with *did* or *didn't*

(WRONG)	Did you gave
(RIGHT)	Did you give

(WRONG)	Didn't you saw
(RIGHT)	Didn't you see

Question Words

Many questions begin with the words *who, whose, whom, which, where, when, why,* or *how.*

> Who is at the door?
> Whom did you see?

In the first question, *who* is the subject of the sentence, so we use the subject form *who.*

In the second question, *you* is the subject of the sentence. The unknown person the subject saw is the object of this sentence, so we use the object form *whom.*

EXERCISE 18: Turn each declarative sentence into a question sentence.

1. This goat eats paper.

_____

2. You heard the cuckoo.

_____

3. My dog came home.

_____

4. Our team has beaten yours.

_____

5. The sun rose at 6 A.M.

_____

6. It doesn't matter.

_____

7. Someone came to the door.

_____

8. This car cost a lot of money.

COMMANDS—Imperative Sentences

An imperative sentence gives a command. It ends with either an exclamation mark or a period. If there is some urgency in the command, use an exclamation mark after the sentence. Otherwise, use a period.

> Don't break it!
> Please, speak slowly.

The imperative or command form of a verb is always its plain form. As for the subjects of imperative sentences, can you find the subjects of the two sentences above?

Imperative sentences have no subjects. They are addressed to whoever is listening. Their unspoken subject is *You, there*.

> (You, there,) Don't break it!
> (You, there,) Please, speak slowly.

EXCLAMATIONS—Exclamatory Sentences

An exclamatory sentence ends with an exclamation mark. Exclamations, just like commands, are incomplete sentences. Commands have no subject. Exclamations have no verb, and either no subject or no subject complement.

> What a beautiful morning!
> How marvelous!
> So unnecessary!

The unspoken part of such sentences is something like *this is*.

> What a beautiful morning (this is)!
> How marvelous (this is)!
> (This is) So unnecessary!

For additional practice, turn to the review test for this chapter at the back of the book.

4. USING THE PARTS OF SPEECH CORRECTLY

Languages are like games. Each has its own rules by which all its users or players have to abide. Knowing the rules helps you to understand exactly what other people mean to convey in speech or in writing. Using the rules yourself allows others to understand exactly what you mean to convey in speech or in writing.

AGREEMENT OF SUBJECT AND VERB

The verb of a sentence must agree with its subject in person and number.

A noun subject is always in the third person. A noun in the singular is third person singular (like *he, she, it*). A noun in the plural is third person plural (like *they*). The reason it matters whether a noun subject is in the singular or plural is that in many tenses the verb form for third person singular is different from the verb form for third person plural.

HE-SHE-IT	THEY
is sitting	are sitting
sits	sit
was sitting	were sitting
has sat	have sat
has been sitting	have been sitting
does not sit	do not sit
doesn't sit	don't sit

EXERCISE 19: Choose the correct verb form in each sentence.

1. The seals (has/have) _____ been barking.

2. (Does/Do) _____ the dogs chew your furniture?

3. Our parrot (has/have) _____ not said a word.

4. (Was/Were) _____ your friends teasing it?

The Verb Must Agree with Its Simple Subject—Not with the Description or Explanation of the Subject

A simple noun subject can be accompanied by words that describe or explain it. To decide whether the subject of the sentence is singular or plural, ignore the descriptions and explanations. All that counts is the simple subject. If the simple subject is in the singular, use the third person singular form of the verb. If the simple subject is in the plural, use the third person plural form of the verb.

> The pink and red *flowers* in the tall vase *have* wilted.
> The old *table* my parents gave us *needs* a coat of paint.
> The back *wheels* of the car you borrowed *are* wobbling.

EXERCISE 20: In each sentence, underline the simple subject and choose the correct verb form.

1. The size of your arm and leg muscles (show/shows) _____ that you are a swimmer.

2. The owner of seventeen dogs (live/lives) _____ next door to me.

3. The story the newspapers printed (sound/sounds) _____ fascinating.

4. My presents for her only child (were/was) _____ wrapped in pink paper.

5. The children's breakfast of toast and scrambled eggs (are/is) _____ ready.

6. The sleeves of your blue coat (do/does) _____ not fit.

7. The room with the thirty-five pen drawings (intrigue/intrigues) _____ me.

8. My parents' and grandparents' idea of fun (are/is) _____ not the same as mine.

The Verb Must Agree with Its Simple Subject—Not with the Subject Complement

The subject and its complement are not always both in the singular or both in the plural. If one is singular and the other plural, the verb should agree with the subject.

> His only *hobby is* his racing pigeons.
> Her *parents are* her sole support.

EXERCISE 21: In each sentence, underline the simple subject and choose the correct verb form.

1. The thing I enjoyed (were/was) _____ the games we played.

2. The cause of his troubles (are/is) _____ his moods.

3. The bear's claws (are/is) _____ its main weapons.

4. In his garden, the roses (have/has) _____ been his special pride.

5. All last winter, the cockroaches (were/was) _____ a terrible pest.

6. Your various illnesses (have/has) _____ been a great handicap.

7. French fried potatoes (were/was) _____ her favorite food.

8. Robert and Suzanne (are/is) _____ a married couple.

Question Sentences

In questions, the subject follows the verb and determines the person and number of the verb form.

> Where in the house *are* the *medicines* kept?
> Why *doesn't* the *soup* have any noodles?
> Under which tree *do* the *mushrooms* grow?

Sentences Starting with Here and There

In such sentences the subject follows the verb and determines the person and number of the verb form.

> Here *is* the famous flea *circus.*
> Here *are* the famous *fleas.*
> There *is* a *mouse* in the attic.
> There *are* *mice* in the attic.

EXERCISE 22: In each sentence, underline the simple subject and choose the correct verb form.

1. Where (has/have) _____ your children's friend gone?

2. (Doesn't/Don't) _____ this artist's pictures please you?

3. There (was/were) _____ some strange-looking outfits for sale.

4. Here (comes/come) _____ the person we all want to meet.

5. There (is/are) _____ beautiful blue grapes in the market.

6. Why (doesn't/don't) _____ our front door bell work?

7. There (is/are) _____ no birds sitting on that tree.

8. How (does/do) _____ bears manage to sleep all winter?

Indefinite Pronoun Subjects

Some indefinite pronouns are always in the singular, and some are always in the plural.

ALWAYS SINGULAR			ALWAYS PLURAL
everybody	everyone	everything	several
somebody	someone	something	many
anybody	anyone	anything	few
nobody	no one	nothing	both
each	one	another	others

Nobody knows her.	Several work here.
Has anyone asked?	Many have done it.
Everyone says so.	Few believe it.
Each gets a ticket.	Both were yellow.
One uses a hammer.	Others disagree.
Another has arrived.	

EXERCISE 23: In each sentence, choose the correct verb form.

1. Everybody (has/have) _____ heard about the twins.

2. Many (sees/see) _____ them in the morning.

3. Each of the boys (rides/ride) —————— a bicycle.

4. Both (has/have) —————— a paper route.

5. Few (knows/know) —————— which twin is which.

6. One (hopes/hope) —————— that does not upset them.

7. (Does/Do) —————— anyone know how to tell them apart?

8. Some (has/have) —————— noticed a difference in their smiles.

Compound Subjects: Do Two Singulars Make a Plural?

Every compound subject has two or more single subjects that are tied together by a conjunction.

> my sister *and* I   the dog *or* the cat
> Jane *or* Bill   *either* the dog *or* the cat
>   *neither* the dog *nor* the cat

When all parts of the compound subject are in the singular, the conjunction that joins them together tells us whether the verb of the sentence must be in the singular or the plural.

Compounds Joined by *And*

When the word *and* ties the single subjects together, the subject consists of at least two people or things. Therefore the subject counts as a plural, and its verb must also be in the plural.

> Jack *goes* up the hill.
> Jack *and* Jill *go* up the hill.

> My hammer *and* saw *are* missing.
> My hammer *and* saw *and* chisel *are* missing.
> My hammer, saw, *and* chisel *are* missing.

> The electric cooker *does* not work.
> The electric cooker *and* light *do* not work.
> The electric cooker, light, *and* wall plug *do* not work.

EXCEPTION 1

When all parts of the compound subject refer to the same person or thing or idea, use a singular form of the verb.

> Our friend, adviser, and benefactor was Mrs. Jones.
> *Androcles and the Lion* was written by Bernard Shaw.
> Coffee and cream is served every morning.
> "Ladies and Gentlemen," is the way to begin a speech.

EXCEPTION 2

If the first part or all parts of the compound subject are preceded by *every* or *each*, that makes us consider each part of the compound separately. Therefore the verb of the sentence must be in the singular.

> Every car and truck needs a license.
> Each graduate and each professor was wearing a cap and gown.
> Does each boy and girl get a balloon?

EXERCISE 24: In each sentence, decide whether the compound subject counts as a singular or a plural, and then choose the correct verb form.

1. Each singer and instrumentalist (was/were) _____ dressed in black.

2. Robert and Jane (wants/want) _____ to buy a monkey.

3. His exercise and sport (is/are) _____ basketball.

4. Every player and every fan (loves/love) _____ this coach.

5. The fans and the players all (hates/hate) _____ this umpire.

6. Pat or Sandy (is/are) _____ going to accompany you.

7. My friend and I (was/were) _____ extremely pleased.

8. Where (does/do) _____ Edgar and Joan live?

Compounds Joined by *Or, Either—Or, Neither—Nor*

When the parts of a compound subject are in the singular and are connected by *or, either–or, neither–nor,* the verb of the sentence must be in the singular.

My brother or my sister has borrowed my keys.
Either Spanish or Portuguese is spoken in South America.
Neither Bolivia nor Paraguay borders on an ocean.

Subjects with Interrupters

The following expressions are interrupters, not conjunctions.

as well as   together with
in addition to   accompanied by

In meaning, they are similar to the conjunction *and,* but they are not the same. Two words that are joined by *and* are both of equal importance. Two words joined by an interrupter are of unequal importance. The first one is really important, and the second one is an afterthought that could just as well be left out.

Chess as well as checkers is played on this board.
Cake in addition to coffee was served.
The bride together with the bridesmaids enters.
The bride accompanied by her father walks up the aisle.

In deciding whether such compound subjects are singular or plural, ignore the part that follows the interrupter. Just look to see whether the first part of the subject is singular or plural, and make the verb agree with that.

EXERCISE 25: In each sentence, choose the correct verb form.

1. The birds and the bees (has/have) _____ taught me a lot.

2. The birds as well as the bees (has/have) _____ taught me a lot.

3. Neither a bird nor a bee ever (teaches/teach) _____ anyone anything.

4. A bird as well as a bee (flies/fly) _____ a lot.

5. A bird accompanied by a bee (is/are) _____ eating my pear.

6. Every bird and bee on my food (is/are) _____ a nuisance.

7. Birds in addition to bees (is/are) _____ attacking my breakfast.

8. Now the bird or the bees (has/have) _____ spilled my coffee.

Collective Noun Subjects

We use such nouns as *orchestra, family, team, group, crowd,* to speak of a group of individuals acting as though they were one. Nouns like these are known as *collective nouns.*

A collective noun in the singular calls for the singular form of the verb.

> The orchestra *travels* in its own bus.
> Orchestras *do* a lot of traveling.
> My family *has* moved to a new house.
> The crowd *was* thrilled.
> Crowds *have* welcomed us in every city.
> The company *has* to pay your insurance.
> The team *doesn't* win very often.

EXCEPTION

When the members of the group don't act as one unit but as separate individuals, use the plural form of the verb.

> The crew *has* much work to do.
> The crew *come* from seven different countries.

Subjects That Identify Part of a Larger Unit

When your subject is *some of the peas* or *most of the cake,* the larger units are *peas* and *cake. Some of* and *most of* indicate the size of the part we are talking about.

The plural or singular of the larger unit determines whether the verb should be in the plural or singular.

> Most of the cake has been eaten.
> Most of the cakes have been eaten.
> Half of the performance was good.
> Half of the performances were good.
> Three quarters of the speech was boring.
> Three quarters of the speeches were boring.
> The rest of the entertainment was fun.
> The rest of the entertainments were fun.

Singulars That Sound like Plurals

Have you ever suffered from a *mump* or a *measle?* Can you study *mathematic* or eat a *molass?*

Measles *is* a disease, and so *is* mumps.

Use the singular form of a verb with words like the following.

mathematics	gymnastics
economics	politics
physics	news
electronics	molasses

EXERCISE 26: In each sentence, choose the correct verb form.

1. Our company (has/have) _____ bought three computers.

2. Electronics (is/are) _____ a mystery to us.

3. Half the people (doesn't/don't) _____ understand it.

4. Most of it (doesn't/don't) _____ interest them.

5. My group (wants/want) _____ to be able to use computers.

6. Most of us (thinks/think) _____ it will further our careers.

7. The economics of business (demands/demand) _____ the use of such machines.

8. Backward companies (is/are) _____ bound to go under.

EXERCISE 27—Subject-Verb Agreement Review: In each sentence, choose the correct verb form.

1. The first dinosaur bones (was/were) _____ found in Wyoming.

2. There (is/are) _____ no living dinosaurs today.

3. The rise of the dinosaurs, as well as their fall, (poses/pose) _____ many unanswered questions.

4. Dinosaurs (is/are) _____ my field of study.

5. Almost everyone (considers/consider) _____ that peculiar.

6. Physics or mathematics (is/are) _____ not regarded as peculiar.

7. Physics and mathematics (does/do) _____ not thrill me at all.

8. My family (has/have) _____ allowed me to follow my own interests.

9. All the members of my family (follows/follow) _____ their own interests.

10. No sport or entertainment (pleases/please) _____ us more than our work.

11. There (is/are) _____ three of us researching natural history.

12. Each of us (specializes/specialize) _____ in a different branch of natural history.

PRONOUN CHOICE

A lot of people slip up when it comes to pronouns. After all the practice in the preceding chapters and all the reviewing that follows now, the correct use of pronouns should be quite clear to you.

Personal Pronouns

If a personal pronoun is the subject, part of a compound subject, or the subject complement, use *I, you, he, she, it, we, they.*

If a personal pronoun is the object or part of the object, use *me, you, him, her, it, us, them.*

Many people slip up when they use a compound subject like *my mother and me/I,* or a compound object like *his uncle and him/he.* Often, the easiest way of finding the right form is to disregard the other part of the compound subject or object.

> (My mother and) *I* went bowling.
> They gave a ride to (my sister and) *me.*
> (Our friends and) *we* left quite early.

EXERCISE 28: In each sentence, choose the correct pronoun form.

1. John and (me/I) _____ went to the movies.

2. The person who won the race was (her/she) _____.

3. This secret is known only by you and (me/I) _____.

4. Barbara and (him/he) _____ liked one another.

5. We and (them/they) _____ will meet on Tuesday.

6. The Smiths and (us/we) _____ are the best of friends.

7. Bill saw my mother and (me/I) _____ do our shopping.

8. He and (her/she) _____ both have the mumps.

9. The only ones here were (him and her/he and she) _____.

10. Terry can sit between you and (me/I) _____.

Reflexive Pronouns

Reflexive pronouns are used to refer back to the subject of the sentence.

> I have seen *myself*.
> You have excelled *yourself*.
> He cut *himself*. (never *hisself*)
> Amy dressed *herself*.
> This oven cleans *itself*.
> We found *ourselves* in a traffic jam.
> The guests will entertain *themselves*. (never *theirselves*)

Reflexive pronouns can also be added to emphasize a pronoun or noun that is already in the sentence.

> *She* told me so *herself*.
> *I myself* spoke to your landlord.
> We approached the *owners themselves*.

Don't use the reflexive pronoun without the antecedent it should refer to.

(WRONG) My father and myself went swimming.
(RIGHT) My father and I went swimming.

(WRONG) Your aunt and yourself must come and visit us.
(RIGHT) You and your aunt must come and visit us.

(WRONG) They liked my friend and myself.
(RIGHT) They liked my friend and me.

Good manners demand that you mention yourself last when you speak of yourself and another person.

My father and I went
gave some to her and me

Good manners demand that you mention the listener (or reader) first when you speak of the listener (or reader) and another person.

You and Emma are welcome
will write to you and him

EXERCISE 29: Choose the correct pronouns for each sentence.

1. John bought (him/himself/hisself) _____ a sweater.
2. I will phone (you and her/her and you/her and yourself)

   _____.

3. They think they found (ourselves/us) _____ an apartment.

4. She would like to see (Alex and me/me and Alex/Alex and myself)

   _____.

5. The children are too young to dress (theirself/themselves)

   _____.

6. We like to spoil others and (ourselves/us) _____.

Possessive Pronouns

Preceding a noun, use *my, your, his, her, its, our, your, their*.

your coat   its buttons

As a subject complement that is not followed by a noun, use *mine, yours, his, hers, ours, yours, theirs* (don't use *its* by itself).

The profit from the farm is *hers*.
If it is *theirs*, it can't be *ours*.

Note that possessive pronouns don't have apostrophes, even when they are formed by adding an *s*.

Demonstrative Pronouns

Using a demonstrative pronoun is like pointing to something without really naming it.

> I want *this*.
> *That* is the dog who bit me.
> Please, give me a pound of *these*.
> *Those* will last you a long time.

Refer to something in the singular with *this* and *that*. Refer to something in the plural with *these* and *those*. Make sure the subject, verb, and subject complement agree in number.

> (WRONG) That was the friends I told you about.
> (RIGHT) Those were the friends I told you about.
> (RIGHT) That was the friend I told you about.

> (WRONG) This is all the apples I could find.
> (RIGHT) These are all the apples I could find.
> (RIGHT) This is all I could find.

The words *this, that, these,* and *those* can also be used as determiners instead of *the* in order to pinpoint something.

> (RIGHT) this table, these chairs
> (WRONG) this here table, these here chairs.

The meaning of *this* and *these* is "the one here" and "the ones here," so *here* is superfluous after *this* and *these*.

> (RIGHT) that camel, those elephants
> (WRONG) that there camel, those there elephants

The meaning of *that* and *those* is "the one there," and "the ones there," so *there* is superfluous immediately after *that* or *those*.

> (RIGHT) Those (or These) books you lent me are good.
> (WRONG) Them books you lent me are good.

Them can never be used in place of *the*.

> (RIGHT) There was an amusement park we went to.
> (WRONG) There was this amusement park we went to.

If you are introducing a new topic of conversation, there is no need to pinpoint anything.

EXERCISE 30: Choose the correct forms for each sentence.

1. (Those were/That was) _____the shoes I wore.

2. (This is/These are) _____ my oldest friends.

3. (This is/These are) _____ my oldest friends' daughter.

4. (Those there is/Those there are/Those are) _____ the most popular records at present.

5. We don't want to offend (these/them) _____ people.

6. There was (this/a) _____ dog I saw in the street.

Relative Pronouns

When we want to give additional information about someone or something mentioned in the sentence, we often use a dependent clause that begins with a relative pronoun.

> The car will be waiting for you.
> The car, *which* is a red, four-door sedan, will be waiting for you.

> We brought home a chair.
> We brought home a chair *that* we found in the street.

Which begins a clause that gives additional information about some thing or things.

That can often be used to begin a clause with additional information about some thing or things.

Who, whom, whose is the beginning of a clause that provides additional information about some person or persons, or about some animal or animals that seem like persons.

Who or Whom?

A dependent clause has its own subject and verb, and it may have an object as well. As subject of the dependent clause, use the relative pronoun *who*. As object of the dependent clause, use the relative pronoun *whom*.

> The owner, who is on vacation, will return next week.

Dependent Clause: *who is on vacation*
Verb of the Dependent Clause: *is*
Subject of the Dependent Clause: *who*

The owner, whom you will meet, will return next week.

Dependent Clause: *whom you will meet*
Verb of the Dependent Clause: *will meet*
Subject of the Dependent Clause: *you*
Object of the Dependent Clause: *whom*

We saw the fellow from whom you bought the dog.

Dependent Clause: *from whom you bought the dog*
Verb of the Dependent Clause: *bought*
Subject of the Dependent Clause: *you*
Preposition and Its Object in the Dependent Clause: *from whom*
Direct Object in the Dependent Clause: *the dog*

EXERCISE 31: With each sentence, copy its dependent clause onto the answer line. Then underline the subject of the clause you copied, and cross out the wrong form of the relative pronoun.

1. My brother, who/whom has no car, needs transportation.

   _____

2. The Johnsons, who/whom everyone hates, are coming.

   _____

3. They had a daughter who/whom they named Rosemary.

   _____

4. The boy, who/whom was named Maximilian, weighs seven pounds.

   _____

5. Sandy, who/whom we had invited, never showed up.

   _____

6. The people to who/whom we gave the keys have disappeared.

   _____

7. The woman who/whom Bob will marry can't cook.

   _____

8. Linda, for who/whom you were waiting, has arrived.

   _____

9. We need a babysitter who/whom we can trust.

---

10. Boris is a dog who/whom barks and eats a lot.

The Possessive of Relative Pronouns

To show possession by a person, persons, or animal(s), use *whose*. (Note the spelling.)

> The dog, *whose* jaws are powerful, cracked the bone.
> We stayed with friends *whose* boiler broke down.

In theory, *of which* shows possession by a thing or things. In practice, you usually get an awkward sentence when you use *of which*. To avoid that, you have two options: use *whose* to show possession by things, or recast your sentence so that you need neither *whose* nor *of which*.

(AWKWARD)	The tree of which the bark has been stripped will die.
(BETTER)	The tree whose bark has been stripped will die.

(AWKWARD)	Sentences of which the length is great are difficult to read.
(BETTER)	Sentences whose length is great are difficult to read.
(BEST)	Sentences of great length are difficult to read.

Prepositions Accompanying Relative Pronouns

Prepositions are frequently used together with *whom, whose,* or *which*. Just about every preposition can be used with *whom, whose,* or *which*.

> This is the girl *on whom* I depend.
> She works for the man *in whose* house we live.
> Show us the brushes *with which* you paint.

Did you notice that *who* was not listed here?

Who is always the subject of a dependent clause. No subject is ever preceded by a preposition. *From the table* or *around the corner* or *beside Terry* could never be subjects. They must always be objects. If you see a dependent clause that begins with a preposition followed by *who*, you know that it's wrong and should be a preposition followed by *whom*.

You can generally choose between two positions for the preposition: immediately before the relative pronoun, or at the end of the dependent clause.

The doctor *to* whose office you went
The doctor whose office you went *to*
The pan *in* which we cook eggs
The pan which we cook eggs *in*
The friends *with* whom I went skating
The friends whom I went skating *with*

In conversation, we often put the preposition at the end of the dependent clause. In writing, it is usually better to put it just before *whom, whose,* or *which.* Choose one position or the other, but never use both in the same clause. It is wrong to say: *The friends with whom I went skating with.*

EXERCISE 32—PRONOUN REVIEW: Some of the following sentences are correct, but many contain a pronoun error. When you find a pronoun error, underline the wrong word, and write the correct pronoun in the blank.

_____   1. They sent a letter to you and I.

_____   2. The boy with who I saw her was her son.

_____   3. Those are the shoes that she bought.

_____   4. Them are the gloves that we found.

_____   5. Will you invite Max and myself?

_____   6. We and them became very good friends.

_____   7. This is the book for which you paid.

_____   8. These are the children for which you cooked.

_____   9. She herself cooked dinner for himself and his mother.

_____   10. We got us some new plants for the living room.

_____   11. The man who bored us kept repeating hisself.

_____   12. Him and his sister have gone for a walk.

_____   13. They saw themself in the mirror.

_____   14. This is the firm whose employees are on strike.

_____   15. She is the dentist to whom he went.

——————— **16.** The woman, who was furious, blamed you and me.

——————— **17.** The dog that you and her found is ours.

——————— **18.** They have reserved seats for ourselves.

——————— **19.** This must be our seats.

——————— **20.** Those seats are too expensive for you and I.

VERB TENSES, VOICES, AND MOODS

What Meanings Do Our Tenses Have?

The tense of a verb indicates in which time frame things are, have been, or will be done, exist, existed, or will exist.

Present Progressive

To indicate that an action is in progress right now, we use the present progressive, which is the *-ing* form of the verb combined with *am, is,* or *are.*

> I am eating pancakes.
> It is snowing here.
> The birds are singing.

Simple Present

To indicate that something is generally true, rather than not true, we use the simple present. This is the plain form of the verb, which needs an additional *s* in the third person singular.

> I eat pancakes.   (I don't refuse to eat them.)
> It snows here.   (It's not too far south for snow here.)
> Birds sing.   (They don't bark or grunt.)
> She has two dogs.   (Not ten dogs or twelve canaries.)

Simple Past

The simple past is used for a one-shot action that began and ended in the past.

> I ate pancakes.
> It snowed here.
> The birds sang.
> She had two dogs.

What the word *simple* means in *simple present* and *simple past* is that these tenses are formed by the verb alone. In these tenses the verb does not need to add any forms of the helping verbs *to be* or *to have*.

Past Progressive

To indicate that an action that began and ended in the past lasted for some time, we use the *-ing* form of the verb together with *was* or *were*. The past progressive is often used to provide the background or explanation for another action in the simple past.

> I was eating pancakes and finished the syrup.
> It was snowing here the day we arrived.
> The birds were singing when you woke up.

Present Perfect

We use the present perfect to indicate that an action began in the past and has either continued to the present time or still affects the present time. The present perfect is formed by the past participle of the verb together with *has* or *have*.

> She has borrowed my book (and hasn't returned it).
> I have eaten there (so I know how well they cook).
> They have studied anatomy (and can tell a biceps from a triceps).
> He has bought a dog (and is its owner now).
> You have met her (so she is no stranger to you).

Past Perfect

We use the past perfect to speak of a past action that was completed before another past action began. The past perfect is formed by the past participle of the verb together with *had*.

> She had bought a flashlight, which I borrowed.
> Our team had won the game, so we celebrated.
> He went by bus because he had wrecked his car.
> I had read a review of the play I saw.
> They had walked a long way and were feeling tired.

Future Tenses

To indicate an action at some time in the future, we use the plain form of the verb together with *will* (or *shall* in the first person) or together with *am/are/is going to.*

>I will/shall travel.
>You will receive my letters.
>It is going to take five minutes.

To indicate an action in the immediate future, we can use the plain form combined with *am/are/is about to.*

>The runners are about to start.

We use the future progressive to indicate a future action that will last for some time. The future progressive consists of the *-ing* form of the verb together with *will/shall be.*

>She will be sleeping when you return.

The future perfect can indicate a future action that is already completed before another future action begins. The future perfect is formed by the past participle of the verb together with *will/shall have.*

>He will have eaten by the time you return.

EXERCISE 33: Some of the following sentences are correct, but many have a verb form error. Underline any wrong form, and write the correct form in the blank.

————— 1. It were not raining yesterday.

————— 2. Some birds sings better than others.

————— 3. She growed a lot last year.

————— 4. We was waiting for you.

————— 5. I have took that horrible medicine.

————— 6. He had forgot your birthday.

————— 7. Someone has stole my grammar book.

————— 8. We would have froze without our coats.

————— 9. You could have caught that ball.

————— 10. I slided down the bannisters.

_____ **11.** This horse has never been ridden.

_____ **12.** She weeped like a fountain.

Voices

What is the difference between *we gave* and *we were given,* between *she saw* and *she was seen?*

In each pair, the first verb is in the active voice and the second verb is in the passive voice. With a verb in the active voice, the subject performs some action. With the verb in the passive voice, the subject receives some action performed by others.

The passive voice uses the past participle of a verb combined with the various forms and tenses of the verb *to be.*

	ACTIVE	PASSIVE
SIMPLE PRESENT	I take	you are taken
SIMPLE PAST	I took	you were taken
PRESENT PERFECT	I have taken	you have been taken
PAST PERFECT	I had taken	you had been taken
FUTURE	I will take	you will be taken
FUTURE PERFECT	I will have taken	you will have been taken

In the active voice, sentences are relatively short and direct. In the passive voice, sentences tend to be vague. If you try to make them less vague, they tend to become relatively long and cumbersome.

(SHORT AND DIRECT)   Raymond took Patricia to the zoo.
(VAGUE)   Patricia was taken to the zoo. (by bus, by you?)
(CUMBERSOME)   Patricia was taken to the zoo by Raymond.

What happens when you change a sentence from active voice to passive voice?

(ACTIVE)   Robert has eaten the pancakes.
(PASSIVE)   The pancakes have been eaten by Robert.

The object of the active sentence (*pancakes*) becomes the subject of the passive sentence. The subject of the active sentence (*Robert*) becomes the object of the preposition *by* in the passive sentence. In each sentence, the verb must agree with its subject. In the active sentence, it must agree with *Robert,* so it is *has,* third person singular. In the passive sentence, it must agree with *pancakes,* so it is *have,* third person plural.

EXERCISE 34: Rewrite the following sentences, but let them keep the same meaning. Change every sentence that has an active verb into one that has a passive verb. Change every sentence that has a passive verb into one with an active verb.

1. The car has been washed and polished by Marc.

   Marc has washed and polished the car.

2. The apple was eaten by you.

3. Our dog was bitten by fleas.

4. Mary has borrowed your radio.

5. Flowers were sent to me for my birthday by somebody.

6. We took the dog for a walk.

7. They bought a round-trip ticket to Seattle.

8. You have not been seen by us for three weeks.

9. Rain followed the thunderstorm.

Moods

A verb can be in one of three moods: the indicative, the imperative, or the subjunctive.

Indicative

All the verb forms we use to state a fact or ask a question are part of the indicative mood.

> This coat looks strange.
> Who gave it to you?

Note that both kinds of sentences have subject and verb.

Imperative

The verb form in a command sentence is the imperative form of the verb. The imperative is the plain form of the verb.

> Look at that coat.
> Give me a chance.
> Be quiet.
> Have some cherries.

Note that in an imperative sentence the subject (*You, there,*) is always missing.

Subjunctive

When we set up a scenario that is quite contrary to reality, we use the subjunctive form *were* instead of the indicative *am, is, are.*

> If I were you   (I am obviously not.)
> If he were a millionaire   (We all know he isn't.)
> If she were living still   (We know she is dead.)

The subjunctive is also used for hypothetical cases.

> (SUBJUNCTIVE)   If I *were* sick, *would* you look after me?
> (INDICATIVE)   I *am* sick. *Will* you look after me?

> (SUBJUNCTIVE)   If she *were* to leave, the firm *would* collapse.
> (INDICATIVE)   She *is* going to leave, and the firm *will* collapse.

> (SUBJUNCTIVE)   If you *were* to play, we *could* win.
> (INDICATIVE)   You *are* going to play, so we *can* win.

Another subjunctive that is used in formal speech or procedure is the plain form of the verb in a phrase beginning with *that.*

> I suggest that they *be* expelled from the club.
> I move that new uniforms *be* acquired.
> I recommend that he *pay* the full amount.
> I request that she *allow* us to attend.

Sentences like the four preceding ones sound quite normal if you insert *should* before the plain form of the verb.

EXERCISE 35: Identify each sentence as being either in the indicative (IND), or in the imperative (IMP), or in the subjunctive (SUB).

_____ 1. Help yourself to some snails and frog legs.

_____ 2. You are a very kind hostess.

_____ 3. If I were not so full, I would certainly help myself.

_____ 4. Run around the block a few times.

_____ 5. I will be back in a little while.

_____ 6. I wouldn't eat snails or frogs if I were offered fifty dollars.

_____ 7. Give me two hot dogs, please.

_____ 8. Here I am back again, but I'm still not hungry.

COMPARISONS

When we use nouns, we identify things or people. By adding adjectives to these nouns, we usually add our own opinion or perception of those things or people.

> The dog found a bone.
> The *old* dog found an *ancient* bone.

In our opinion, this dog was old in relation to dogs in general, and this bone was ancient in relation to bones in general.

When we use action verbs, we identify the performing of actions. By adding adverbs to these verbs, we can add our opinion of the manner in which those actions were performed.

> The dog barked.
> The dog barked *loudly* and *often*.

In relation to other dogs we have known, this dog's bark was noisy and frequent.

The first degree of comparison consists of using the plain adjective or adverb. It compares a specific thing or action to others which are not named.

The second degree of comparison consists of saying the *older* dog, a *more ancient* bone, and barked *more loudly* and *more often*. This second degree of comparison is called the *comparative*.

The third degree of comparison consists of saying the *oldest* dog, the *most ancient* bone, and barked *most loudly* and *most often*. This third degree of comparison is known as the *superlative*.

The Uses of Comparatives and Superlatives

To whom or to what you compare something determines whether you should use the comparative or use the superlative. One will be right, the other wrong.

Comparative

When you compare something to one other thing or action, or to one other group of things or actions, use the comparative.

> Tweedledum is nicer than Tweedledee.
> Mice are smaller than rats.
> Mice eat less than rats.
> She speaks more distinctly than he.
> Elephants move more slowly than cheetahs.

Sometimes the other thing, action, or group of things or actions is not mentioned but understood in the context in which it occurs.

> Please speak more distinctly (than you did before).
> We can see farther now (than before).
> These shoes are larger (than the others).

Superlative

When you compare something to more than one other thing or action, or to more than one group of things or actions, use the superlative.

> Who is the smartest of your ten students?
> You are the most successful member of our team.
> That is the worst team in the league.
> It was the funniest story in the book.
> He shouted most loudly of all.
> I like you best of all my friends.

When we use the superlative merely for emphasis, we don't necessarily spell out the whole comparison. If you added *of all you can imagine,* or *of all the ways it could be done,* such comparisons would be complete.

> Frank is the greatest singer.
> It was the most enormous balloon.
> She fell most awkwardly.

Comparing with Adjectives

Some adjectives form their comparatives and superlatives with *-er* and *-est*.

small	smaller	smallest
noisy	noisier	noisiest
friendly	friendlier	friendliest
feeble	feebler	feeblest

Other adjectives form their comparatives and superlatives with *more* and *most.*

awful	more awful	most awful
marvelous	more marvelous	most marvelous
specific	more specific	most specific

How can you tell which ones use *-er* and *-est* and which use *more* and *most?*

Adjectives of one syllable use *-er* and *-est.* The following two-syllable adjectives also use *-er* and *-est*: those whose second syllable ends in *y, ow,* or consonant plus *le.* All other adjectives use *more* and *most.*

quick	quicker	quickest
nice	nicer	nicest
pretty	prettier	prettiest
lively	livelier	liveliest
hollow	hollower	hollowest
simple	simpler	simplest
acid	more acid	most acid
hideous	more hideous	most hideous
harmless	more harmless	most harmless
useful	more useful	most useful
cordial	more cordial	most cordial
futile	more futile	most futile
remarkable	more remarkable	most remarkable

The last two adjectives end in -le, so why don't they use -er and -est?

The second syllable of *futile* ends in vowel plus *le,* not consonant plus *le;* and *remarkable* has four syllables, not two.

With adjectives that use -er and -est, it is not only superfluous but also wrong to use *more* or *most* in addition.

(WRONG)	a more quicker result
(RIGHT)	a quicker result
(WRONG)	the most friendliest dog in the world
(RIGHT)	the friendliest dog in the world
(WRONG)	a more yellower paint
(RIGHT)	a yellower paint
(WRONG)	the most subtlest hint
(RIGHT)	the subtlest hint

Irregular Adjectives

There is a handful of adjectives that use neither -er, -est nor *more, most* to form their comparatives and superlatives. They use totally different words.

good	better	best
bad	worse	worst
many	more	most
much	more	most
little	less	least (quantity)
little	smaller	smallest (size)

It is both superfluous and wrong to use *more* and *most* together with these irregular comparatives and superlatives.

(WRONG)	a more better day than today
(RIGHT)	a better day than today
(WRONG)	the most worst that could happen
(RIGHT)	the worst that could happen

EXERCISE 36: Fill in the comparatives and superlatives of the following adjectives.

1. green _____ _____
2. bad _____ _____
3. funny _____ _____
4. gorgeous _____ _____
5. hopeless _____ _____
6. ample _____ _____
7. truthful _____ _____
8. many _____ _____
9. narrow _____ _____
10. basic _____ _____
11. faint _____ _____
12. afraid _____ _____
13. humble _____ _____
14. brainy _____ _____

Comparatives and Superlatives in Negative Comparisons

An elephant is *less enormous* than a whale.
This was the *least important* of my reasons.
Turtles are *less lively* than gerbils.
You are the *least secretive* person I know.

In such negative comparisons, all adjectives keep their original form. The original form is preceded by *less* in the comparative, and by *least* in the superlative.

It is not only superfluous but also wrong to use the *-er* or *-est* form together with *less* or *least*.

(WRONG) less nicer than before
(RIGHT) less nice than before

(WRONG) the least roundest of the planet's moons
(RIGHT) the least round of the planet's moons

(WRONG)   less better than mine
(RIGHT)   less good than mine

(WRONG)   the least ablest runner
(RIGHT)   the least able runner

EXERCISE 37: Rewrite every sentence correctly. There is an error in every sentence. Watch out for a wrongly formed comparative or superlative. Watch out for a superlative where a comparative should be used. Watch out for a comparative where a superlative should be used.

1. The diamonds were the most tiny you ever saw.

   _____

2. She was the youngest of the two.

   _____

3. My fingers are more stickier than yours.

   _____

4. He had the most worst manners imaginable.

   _____

5. She is less friendlier than you.

   _____

6. This is the acidest vinegar you ever tasted.

   _____

7. These are the thicker of all your socks.

   _____

8. This is a worst handwriting than mine.

   _____

9. You are the most bright person I ever met.

   _____

10. I had the horriblest dream last night.

    _____

Comparing with Adverbs

We can use adverbs to comment on the way an action is carried out.

They think *quickly*.
You smiled *brightly*.

We can also compare the manner in which such actions are carried out.

They think *more quickly* than I.
They think *more quickly* than they write.
They think the *most quickly* of all.
They think *most quickly* when they are in danger.

You smiled *more brightly* than he.
You smiled *more brightly* than you meant to.
You smiled *most brightly* of all.

Adverbs that have been formed by adding *-ly* to an adjective use *more* and *most* to form the comparative and superlative.

true	truly	more/most truly
fond	fondly	more/most fondly
busy	busily	more/most busily
enormous	enormously	more/most enormously
needless	needlessly	more/most needlessly
successful	successfully	more/most successfully
near	nearly	more/most nearly

How about *early*? Why do we speak of leaving *earlier* or *earliest*, and not *more early* or *most early*?

Ask yourself whether *ear* is an adjective.

Adverbs that form their comparatives and superlatives with *-er, -est* are *early, late, hard, long, fast, low,* and *high*. These are words that can be used either as adverbs or as adjectives.

finished early	early bird
stayed late	late arrival
worked hard	hard candy
took long	long trip
drove fast	fast lane
scored low	low ceiling
jumped high	high tide

In comparisons, these adverbs/adjectives follow the adjective rules. They have only one syllable or two syllables ending in *-y*, so they use *-er, -est*.

It would be both superfluous and wrong to use *more* or *most* in addition to *-er, -est*.

(WRONG) he worked more harder
(RIGHT) he worked harder

(WRONG) we drove most fastest
(RIGHT) we drove fastest

Irregular Adverbs

A handful of adverbs use neither *-er, -est* nor *more, most* to form their comparatives and superlatives. They use entirely different words.

well	better	best
badly	worse	worst
ill	worse	worst
much	more	most
little	less	least
far	farther	farthest	(distance)
far	further	furthest	(degree)

It is superfluous and also wrong to add *more* or *most* to these irregular comparatives and superlatives.

(WRONG) Binoculars enable you to see more farther.
(RIGHT) Binoculars enable you to see farther.

(WRONG) The team played most worst in the finals.
(RIGHT) The team played worst in the finals.

EXERCISE 38: Complete each sentence with the adverb and degree of comparison in parentheses.

1. They behaved _____.

   (*foolishly*, superlative)

2. She ate _____ than he.

   (*little*, comparative)

3. We were greeted _____.

   (*politely*, superlative)

4. I will explain it _____.

   (*far*, comparative)

5. He fought _____,

   (*fairly*, superlative)

6. She sang _____ than ever.

   (*atrociously*, comparative)

7. It rained _____ than yesterday.

   (*hard*, comparative)

8. We have studied this _____.

   (*thoroughly*, superlative)

Using As–As in Comparisons

We can use *as–as* for stating that an adjective does or does not apply equally to two nouns or pronouns.

> Janet is as reliable as Laura (is).
> You were as busy as he (was).
> Chickens are not as intelligent as cats (are).
> His bags were not as heavy as mine (were/are).

We can use *as–as* for stating that an adverb does or does not apply equally to the performing of two actions.

> She sings as horribly as she whistles.
> He works as quickly as I (work).
> Geese don't sleep as soundly as bears (sleep).
> He doesn't read as much as he should (read).

A personal pronoun at the end of an *as–as* comparison is often in its subject form.

> You were as busy as *he* (was).
> He works as quickly as *I* (work).

In both cases, the end pronoun is the subject of the missing verb you see in parentheses.

In the following sentence, the end pronoun is in its object form.

Mark likes him as much as (he likes) *her*.

In this case, the end pronoun is the object of the missing verb in parentheses. Whenever you use a pronoun at the end of any comparison, ask yourself whether a part of the complete comparison is missing. If so, figure out what that part is. Then ask yourself whether the end pronoun would be the subject or the object of the missing verb, and use the corresponding pronoun form.

Using Like in Comparisons

We use *like* to say that something does or does not resemble something else.

> This umbrella leaks like a sieve.
> I ate like a horse.
> We hopped like frogs.
> My brother looks like me. (not *I*)
> She behaved like him. (not *he*)
> It did not sound like her. (not *she*)
> They were not dressed like us. (not *we*)
> Like us, they were not dressed.
> Their children are not like them. (not *they*)
> These people don't act like grownups.

In such comparisons, the word *like* is a preposition. The noun or pronoun after *like* is the object of the preposition *like*. Therefore a personal pronoun after *like* must be in its object form: *me, you, him, her, it, us, you, them.*

EXERCISE 39: Choose the correct personal pronoun in each of the following sentences.

1. Their dogs look like (they/them) _____.

2. My brother was as hungry as (I/me) _____.

3. Snails do not move as slowly as (she/her) _____.

4. He cannot skate as fast as (we/us) _____.

5. She talked like (he/him) _____.

6. Like (I/me) _____, they hesitated.

7. Like (he/him) _____, she was a good dancer.

8. She was as good a dancer as (he/him) _____.

SHOULD AN ADVERB OR ADJECTIVE ACCOMPANY THIS VERB?

Adverbs accompany action verbs; they comment on the performing of an action.

> They spoke seriously.

Adjectives accompany linking verbs; they describe the subject, which may be a pronoun, a noun, or a word that functions as a noun.

> They seemed serious.
> George looked serious.
> The quarreling sounded serious.

The linking verb used most often is *to be* in all its forms. *To be* is a linking verb when it stands on its own. It is not a linking verb when it helps to form the tenses of action verbs.

> They have been quick and efficient.
> They have been working quickly and efficiently.

The other linking verbs are the following.

seem	sound	feel
become	smell	stay
appear	taste	grow
remain	look	

The one that can only be used as a linking verb is *seem*. The other ten can either function as linking verbs or as action verbs. As linking verbs they are accompanied by adjectives. As action verbs they are accompanied by adverbs.

(LINKING)	You sounded loud.
(ACTION)	You sounded the bell loudly.

(LINKING)	They tasted suspicious.
(ACTION)	They tasted the soup suspiciously.

(LINKING)	He looked furious.
(ACTION)	He looked furiously for his key.

(LINKING)   She remained glad.
(ACTION)   She gladly remained in order to help him.

(LINKING)   He appeared dead.
(ACTION)   He appeared suddenly.

To test whether one of these verbs is functioning as a linking verb in a sentence, substitute *seemed* for the verb. If the sentence makes sense with *seemed,* the verb was used as a linking verb. If the sentence does not make sense with *seemed,* the verb was used as an action verb.

He looked furious.
He seemed furious.   (makes sense)

He furiously looked for his key.
He furiously seemed for his key.   (makes no sense)

EXERCISE 40: Identify the verb of each sentence as either a linking verb (L) or as an action verb (A).

_____ **1.** The meaning became clear.

_____ **2.** The flowers smelled wonderful.

_____ **3.** They stayed with their grandparents.

_____ **4.** This carpet looks old.

_____ **5.** He appeared unexpectedly at 6 P.M.

_____ **6.** I smelled some wonderful perfume.

_____ **7.** They stayed angry for days.

_____ **8.** Detectives look for clues.

_____ **9.** The crowd remained enthusiastic.

_____ **10.** We grow string beans here.

_____ **11.** String beans grow quickly.

_____ **12.** The gravy remained in the dish.

_____ **13.** Our guests grew sleepy.

_____ **14.** Your soup tasted marvelous.

_____ **15.** Trumpets sounded from the balcony.

_____ **16.** My coat feels wet.

_____ **17.** Your uncle tasted the marvelous soup.

_____ **18.** His story sounds unbelievable.

_____ **19.** Her objections appear silly.

_____ **20.** I felt the edge of the table.

Only adverbs can comment on the performing of an action as expressed by an action verb. Adjectives cannot do that.

> (WRONG) She cooks good.
> (RIGHT) She cooks well.
>
> (WRONG) We played bad.
> (RIGHT) We played badly.
>
> (WRONG) They treated him nice.
> (RIGHT) They treated him nicely.

Adjectives don't comment on action verbs; they comment on nouns or pronouns. Linking verbs allow us to comment on the noun or pronoun subject of a sentence. Therefore adjectives are used after linking verbs.

> (WRONG) It tastes sweetly.
> (RIGHT) It tastes sweet.
>
> (WRONG) You look attractively.
> (RIGHT) You look attractive.

Good or Well and Bad or Badly

Good and _bad_ are always adjectives and can never be used to describe an action verb. Use _well_ and _badly_ to describe an action verb. _Badly_ is always an adverb. _Well_ can be an adverb meaning _properly_ or _nicely_, or it can be an adjective meaning _healthy_.

> I feel well. (adjective [_healthy_] with linking verb)
> You look well. (adjective [_healthy_] with linking verb)
> We slept well. (adverb [_properly_] with action verb)
> She sang well. (adverb [_nicely_] with action verb)

EXERCISE 41: Complete each sentence with the correct word.

1. I hear you (good/well) _____.

2. They argue (endless/endlessly) _____.

3. This chicken tastes (delicious/deliciously) _____.

4. The illness didn't seem (serious/seriously) _____.

5. She certainly dances (good/well) _____.

6. Now she is dancing (quicker/more quickly) _____.

7. The rain was (sudden/suddenly) _____.

8. Last night I slept rather (bad/badly) _____.

9. Could you express yourself (clearer/more clearly) _____?

10. The red apples taste (sweeter/more sweetly) _____.

11. Look at his signature (closer/more closely) _____.

12. They are people who act (quick/quickly) _____.

13. The audience grew (restless/restlessly) _____.

14. The old man will advise you (good/well) _____.

15. The news you brought us sounds (bad/badly) _____.

16. They put the fire out (quick/quickly) _____.

17. On Sundays we dress (formal/formally) _____.

18. In my opinion, it looks (terrible/terribly) _____.

19. I noticed that he read (slow/slowly) _____.

20. Maybe he couldn't see (good/well) _____.

For additional practice, turn to the review test for this chapter at the back of the book.

5. WORDS THAT GET SPECIAL TREATMENT

These words are like any others when we speak. In writing, however, they have to be equipped with signposts for the reader. We will examine two types of signposts: apostrophes and capital letters. Capital letters might be compared to the red-carpet treatment. Apostrophes might be compared to small tombstones.

CONTRACTIONS

There are words we keep using as pairs, and sometimes we don't pronounce both words separately. Between them, the two can form one word known as a *contraction*. In a contraction, the second word loses its vowel.

I am	=	I'm	is not =	isn't
you are	=	you're	are not =	aren't
he is	=	he's	was not =	wasn't
she is	=	she's	were not =	weren't
it is	=	it's	has not =	hasn't
we are	=	we're	have not =	haven't
you are	=	you're	does not =	doesn't
they are	=	they're	do not =	don't
			did not =	didn't
			would not =	wouldn't
			could not =	couldn't
			should not =	shouldn't
			dare not =	daren't

In writing, we mark the place of the lost letter by putting an apostrophe there instead.

With some contractions, the second word loses more than a vowel. As second parts of a contraction, the words *have, has, had, will, would* become *-'ve, -'s, -'d, -'ll, -'d*. In place of the missing letters, we put an apostrophe.

89

I have = I've
you have = you've
he has = he's (same as *he's = he is*)
she has = she's (same as *she's = she is*)
it has = it's (same as *it's = it is*)
we have = we've
you have = you've
they have = they've

I had = I'd	I will = I'll
you had = you'd	you will = you'll
he had = he'd	he will = he'll
she had = she'd	she will = she'll
it had = (no contraction)	it will = it'll
we had = we'd	we will = we'll
you had = you'd	you will = you'll
they had = they'd	they will = they'll

I would = I'd (the same as *I'd = I had*)
you would = you'd (the same as *you'd = you had*)
he would = he'd (the same as *he'd = he had*)
it would   (no contraction)
we would = we'd (the same as *we'd = we had*)
you would = you'd (the same as *you'd = you had*)
they would = they'd (the same as *they'd = they had*)

The contractions of personal pronouns plus *had* look and sound the same as the contractions of personal pronouns plus *would*. Our knowledge of the English language tells us whether *had* or *would* are meant. Let's take two examples.

    (1)   we'd go
    (2)   we'd gone

(1) *Had* or *would? We had go* does not exist, but *we would go* does. So here the *-'d* stands for *would*.
(2) *Had* or *would? We would gone* does not exist, but *we had gone* does. So here the *-'d* stands for *had*.

He, she, it in contractions with *is* look and sound the same as *he, she, it* in contractions with *has*. The context will tell us which one is meant.

    (3)   She's frightened him.
    (4)   She's frightened by him.

(3) *She is frightened him* does not exist, but *she has frightened him* does. So here the *-'s* stands for *has*.
(4) *She has frightened by him* does not exist, but *she is frightened by him* does. So here the *-'s* stands for *is*.

Finally, there are three more contractions with *not* that lose or change more than one letter. In each, an apostrophe replaces the *o* of *not*.

> shall not = shan't
> will not = won't
> cannot = can't (or can not)

More Contractions

Other words that can form contractions together with *is* or *has* are nouns, question words, indefinite pronouns, and words like *here, there, that.*

> Bob is your uncle = Bob's your uncle
> your uncle has gone = your uncle's gone
> who is outside = who's outside
> what has happened = what's happened
> here is the house = here's the house
> there has been a mistake = there's been a mistake
> that has been done = that's been done

A noun, question word, or indefinite pronoun that ends in a vowel sound can also form a contraction with *had* or *would,* as can the word *there.*

> Paula had gone = Paula'd gone
> the sparrow would fly = the sparrow'd fly
> who had taken it = who'd taken it
> how would you go = how'd you go
> somebody had laughed = somebody'd laughed
> nobody would cry = nobody'd cry
> there had been thunder = there'd been thunder
> there would be dinner = there'd be dinner

EXERCISE 42: Each sentence has two words that you should rewrite as a contraction.

1. They are surprised. _____
2. He is amazed. _____

3. She is thunderstruck. _____

4. It is unbelievable. _____

5. Who would have thought it! _____

6. We can not deny it. _____

7. I could not have dreamed it. _____

8. I was not sleeping. _____

9. I have not slept a wink all week. _____

10. You have been exaggerating. _____

11. That is a fact. _____

12. We had suspected that. _____

13. I shall not tell Bob. _____

14. Bob will not keep his mouth shut. _____

15. Bob is a great gossip. _____

16. Do not mention it to Mary. _____

17. Mary would be upset. _____

18. We dare not upset her. _____

19. I will tell Alex. _____

20. Here is the telephone. _____

Contractions That Sound like Possessive Pronouns

Certain contractions sound like certain possessive pronouns, but they don't look alike.

> *They're* washing *their* car.
> We think *it's* a pity the shop raised *its* prices.
> Perhaps *there's* no difference between *theirs* and ours.
> I know *you're* going to meet *your* brother.
> Tell me *who's* borrowed *whose* umbrella.

What obvious difference do you see between the pronouns on the right and the contractions on the left?

Possessive pronouns never have an apostrophe. Contractions always have an apostrophe to mark the place where one or more letters have dropped out.

In writing, you must distinguish between contractions and possessive pronouns. You can easily tell whether it's right or wrong to use the contraction. Just ask yourself which two words made up that contraction. If those two words make sense in your sentence, use the contraction. If not, use the possessive pronoun form.

> The house is theirs/there's.
> The house is there is.   (no sense)
> The house is theirs.

EXERCISE 43: In each sentence, choose the spelling that makes sense.

1. You want my parents, but (their/they're) _____ out.

2. (Its/It's) _____ quite likely they'll be back soon.

3. If (your/you're) _____ not in a hurry, come in.

4. Sit down if (your/you're) _____ feet are tired.

5. (Theirs/There's) _____ a magazine on the table.

6. Look through (its/it's) _____ photographs.

7. (Whose/Who's) _____ faces do you recognize?

8. You found my parents and (their/they're) _____ friends.

9. The donkey you see is (theirs/there's) _____ .

10. I don't know (whose/who's) _____ riding it.

11. (Its/It's) _____ owners would know.

12. I hope you will see (their/they're) _____ garden.

13. (Your/You're) _____ without a car?

14. My parents will pick you up in (theirs/there's) _____ .

15. (Their/They're) _____ grateful for all the favors you do them.

16. Where is (your/you're) _____ own car?

17. (Whose/Who's) _____ borrowed it?

18. That's someone (whose/who's) _____ brother I know.

19. (Its/It's) _____ time we ended this exercise.

20. (Theirs/There's) _____ no point in going on forever.

To Use or Not to Use Contractions

Contractions should not be used in formal writing, such as business correspondence, reports, applications, or requests. Contractions are a way of saving ourselves trouble by pronouncing fewer syllables. In formal writing, we should not give the impression that we are trying to save ourselves some trouble. Furthermore, you know that some contractions are *ambiguous,* which means, they can be interpreted in more than one way. For instance, *she's* could be *she is* or *she has,* and *he'd* could be *he would* or *he had.* Formal writing should never be ambiguous. It should be as clear as possible. So that is another reason why contractions are not appropriate in formal writing.

Now you may wonder why you had to spend so much effort on writing contractions correctly. There are two excellent reasons. (1) You need not and should not be formal when you write to your family, friends, or acquaintances. (2) If you want to write dialogue or quote what people actually said, you should know how to write contractions. We all use a lot of contractions in everyday life.

THE POSSESSIVE FORM OF NOUNS

Suppose Mrs. Smith owns a parrot and you want to refer to that fact. You can use a preposition and say, "the parrot *of* Mrs. Smith." You can use a possessive pronoun and say, "*her* parrot," if Mrs. Smith has just been mentioned. If not, you can use the possessive form of the noun and say, "Mrs. *Smith's* parrot."

The possessive form of a noun always has an apostrophe. In a contraction, the apostrophe shows where one or more letters have dropped out. In the possessive form, the apostrophe shows exactly the same thing. The possessive ending for nouns in the singular used to be *-es* in Old English. Now it is only *-'s* or *-',* so here too, the apostrophe marks the place of the missing letter or letters.

In the singular, all nouns form the possessive by adding *-'s*

Laura's canary   a cousin's teeth
this boss's beard   this actress's costume

In the plural, all regular nouns form the possessive by adding only *-'.* Regular nouns are the nouns that form their plural by adding *-s* or *-es.*

the Robinsons' canary   those cousins' teeth
both bosses' beards   these actresses' costumes

Noun plurals that do not end in *-s* form the possessive by adding *-'s.*

men's coats   children's socks
women's dresses   oxen's yoke

EXERCISE 44: Identify each noun form in italics as either an ordinary singular (OS) or an ordinary plural (OP) or as the possessive form of the singular (PS) or the possessive form of the plural (PP).

1. the *family's* animals _____
2. the *animals* of the family _____
3. *families* with animals _____
4. an animal in the *grass* _____
5. *grasses* in the *animals'* diet _____ _____
6. a *man's* foot _____
7. the *child's* toys _____
8. the *children's* new *toy* _____
9. catching *buses* _____
10. the *bus's* wheels _____
11. the *buses'* drivers _____
12. the *horses'* stable _____
13. the *horse's* nose _____
14. *gases* like hydrogen _____
15. the *gas's* temperature _____
16. *Washington's* art *museums* _____ _____
17. Anthony *Bliss's* name _____
18. *Monday's* concert _____
19. concerts on *Mondays* _____
20. the *museum's* concerts _____

Joint Ownership

The ownership or authorship of a thing is sometimes shared by several people. If you mention these people separately, put only the last of them in the possessive form.

Gilbert and Sullivan's operas
Harcourt Brace Jovanovich's books
Sears, Roebuck's catalog
his aunt and uncle's youngest child
Fred, Ted, and Anna's gift
my brother and sister-in-law's house

EXERCISE 45: In each sentence, choose the correct noun form.

1. She lives by the (rivers/river's/rivers') ＿＿＿＿＿＿ edge.

2. He sat in the (drivers/driver's/drivers') ＿＿＿＿＿＿ seat.

3. Look at the (childrens/children's) ＿＿＿＿＿＿ toys.

4. There are some (cups/cup's/cups') ＿＿＿＿＿＿ on the shelf.

5. All their (books/book's/books') ＿＿＿＿＿＿ covers are torn.

6. Both (glasses/glass's/glasses') ＿＿＿＿＿＿ rims are chipped.

7. Both (parents/parent's/parents') ＿＿＿＿＿＿ worship him.

8. The (Russians/Russian's/Russians') ＿＿＿＿＿＿ Sputnik was the first spacecraft.

9. The (teams/team's/teams') ＿＿＿＿＿＿ mascot is a chimpanzee.

10. (Sailboats/Sailboat's/Sailboats') ＿＿＿＿＿＿ masts are made of wood.

11. A (donkeys/donkey's/donkeys') ＿＿＿＿＿＿ ears are long and furry.

12. All (elephants/elephant's/elephants') ＿＿＿＿＿＿ ears are huge and floppy.

13. A (womans/woman's/womans') ＿＿＿＿＿＿ voice is higher than a (mans/man's/mans') ＿＿＿＿＿＿ .

14. (Womens/Women's/Womens') ＿＿＿＿＿＿ voices are lower than (babies/baby's/babies') ＿＿＿＿＿＿ voices.

15. My (mothers and fathers/mother's and father's/mother and father's) ＿＿＿＿＿＿ home is in Ohio.

16. My (mothers and fathers/mother's and father's/mother and father's)

    _____ toothbrushes are in the bathroom.

17. Your (sister-in-laws/sister-in-law's) _____ baby
    is hungry.

18. All three (sisters/sister's/sisters') _____ hus-
    bands were present.

19. The (husbands/husband's/husbands') _____ of
    all three sisters were present.

20. My (husbands/husband's/husbands') _____ nose
    is running.

CAPITALIZATION

"What's in a name?" asks Shakespeare's Romeo. We have a very safe
answer for Romeo, and that is: *"A capital letter."*

There are two basic sets of rules for capitalization. One set covers
sentences. The other set covers non-sentences such as headlines, headings, and the titles of long or short pieces of writing. The difference
between the two sets could be very roughly summed up as follows:
*In sentences, you capitalize their first word and any name they contain.
In non-sentences, you capitalize almost everything.*

The capitalization of non-sentences will help us with the capitalization of names within sentences, so we will start with non-sentences.
Before we go into the details, though, it should be quite clear what is
meant by *capitalization*. If the rules demand that a word be capitalized,
it means that the word's first letter should be a capital letter. It does not
mean that all its letters should be capitals.

Non-Sentences

Books, articles, and reports have titles and headings that are supposed
to catch the reader's attention. They are not supposed to be or look like
sentences, and 99.9 percent of them are just words or phrases. In writing,
three means are used to make them look different from the regular text.
(1) They occupy a special position on the page. (2) They never end with
a period. (3) They capitalize words that would never be capitalized in a
regular sentence.

Since almost everything is capitalized in a heading or title, it will
be easiest to learn which words don't get a capital in such non-sentences.

The Rules

Don't capitalize the following unless they are the first or the last word of the heading or title.

- The articles *an, a, the*
- The conjunctions *and, or*
- Any preposition of less than five letters

These three classes of words are not considered important enough for capitals unless they are the first or the last word of the title or heading. Why, then, are they capitalized as first or last word of a title or heading? The reason for that is a visual one. A heading or title would look weaker and less complete if its first or last word began with a small letter. For similar visual reasons a preposition of five or more letters is capitalized, even if it is not the first or last word.

Before you go on to the illustrations that follow, refresh your knowledge of prepositions by reading through the list of prepositions on page 28. Then look at the capitalization in the imaginary titles or headings below. All words that are in themselves too unimportant to capitalize are shown in italics.

(1) *On the* Trail *of the* Land *or* Garden Snail
(2) Two Pairs *of* Tentacles *on* Its Head
(3) *The* Shell It Lives *In*
(4) *A* Species That Is Eaten *in* Europe
(5) Things *to* Eat Snails *With*
(6) Snails *with* Toast *and* Garlic Butter
(7) Eating Snails *Between* Meals
(8) *A* Snail *Without a* Shell

In (1), *on* is the first word and is therefore capitalized. Note that *on* is not capitalized in (2). In (3), *the* and *in* are capitalized because one is the first and the other the last word. In (4), *a* is the first word and therefore capitalized. In (5), *with* is the last word and therefore capitalized. Note that *with* is not capitalized in (6). In (7), *between* has five or more letters, so it is capitalized although it is a preposition and neither begins nor ends the title or heading. In (8), *a* is capitalized at the beginning but not in the middle of the title or heading.

EXERCISE 46: Go to page 28 of this book, and copy every preposition you would not capitalize in a title or heading unless it is its first or last word. Then add to your list the three articles and two conjunctions that are not capitalized in a title or heading unless they are in first or last position.

Dashes or Colons in Headings or Titles

A heading or title containing a dash or colon has two parts: one part before the dash or colon, and one part that follows the dash or colon. Each part must begin with a capital letter.

> Solomon—The Wisest of Men
> National Parks: A Guide to Yellowstone Park
> Fare Increases—By January or February

EXERCISE 47: Assume that each of the following lines is a heading or title. Underline the first letter of every word that should be capitalized.

1. gifted and moving into the realm of success
2. signed on with the team for a bonus
3. on the verge of being a free agent
4. something to work and hope for
5. the difference it may or should make
6. rumbling beneath the surface
7. a friend to be with
8. dealing with coaches over the years
9. thinking it over
10. when the contract is up
11. moving farther up the ladder
12. the team that he leaves
13. leaving it without leadership
14. viewing it from a new perspective
15. while he is thinking it over
16. phone calls and offers by the dozen
17. things to look forward to
18. plans for changes in the very near future
19. as far as he can see
20. stardom—the million-dollar contract
21. his record: a series of home runs
22. the end of the story

Sentences

We have become very sparing in our use of capitals within the sentence. If you looked at a book printed two hundred years ago, it would amaze you how many capitals there are in its sentences. Nowadays, capitals in the regular text are mainly used for two purposes: to mark the beginning of a sentence, and to mark the name of a particular person or thing.

The Rules

- Capitalize the first word of every sentence.

- If a complete sentence is quoted within another sentence, capitalize the first word of each sentence.

    > A voice behind her said, "Give me your pearls."
    > She spun around and screamed, "Help!"
    > A yell of "Be quiet!" came from an open window.

- Capitalize all names.

- Capitalize all religions, their adherents, their adjectives.

- Capitalize political parties and their adherents.

- Capitalize nationality and local origin.

- Capitalize the days of the week, the months, religious and national holidays.

Names

You are a *man* or a *woman* who lives in a *house* that is on a *street,* which is in a *city* within a *state* that belongs to a *country.* All these are common nouns, which are not capitalized unless they begin a sentence. A common noun identifies the kind of person(s) or thing(s) we are talking about.

You are *Max Moore* or *Wendy Williams,* who lives in *Highland Towers* on *West Wind Boulevard* in *Chicago,* which is in *Illinois* and belongs to the *United States of America.* All these nouns are proper nouns, or names, which are always capitalized. Each one identifies a particular person or thing.

People's Names and Titles

Capitalize any name that is used to address a particular individual. Everybody has more of such names than just a first and last name. Let's take *Max Moore* as an example.

Some people may address him as *Mister (Mr.) Moore.* If he is a professor, people will call him *Professor Moore.* If he is a doctor, they will call him *Doctor (Dr.) Moore.* When he is elected a councilman, mayor, congressman, or a senator, he will be addressed as *Councilman Moore, Mayor Moore, Congressman Moore,* or *Senator Moore.* He may, however, become a comptroller, attorney general, or a judge, in which case he would be addressed as *Comptroller Moore, Attorney General Moore,* or *Judge Moore.*

Note in the preceding paragraph that the profession or office a person may hold is not capitalized when it stands by itself and identifies a kind of profession or office. Only as part of a person's name, in the form that is used to address the person, do you capitalize the professional title along with the person's last name.

> Dear Professor Moore,
> He was my professor last year.
>
> Dear Doctor Moore,
> This doctor makes house calls.
>
> We will introduce you to Mayor Max Moore.
> Moore, our new mayor, opened the fair.
>
> Maybe Senator Moore could help us.
> He is the junior senator of this state.
>
> The case was heard before Judge Max Moore.
> Moore is a judge of the appeals court.

Note that a noun preceded by a determiner or a possessive pronoun is functioning as a common noun, not as part of somebody's name.

People who write or speak to Moore in his professional capacity may sometimes address him by his professional title only, using his title as if it were his name. In such cases, and such cases only, is the title capitalized although it is not followed by a proper name.

> Dear Professor,
> Dear Comptroller,
> Tell me, Doctor, will I live?
> Allow us, Councilman, to show you the plans.
> It is an honor to welcome you, Mr. Mayor.

Now consider the names by which Max Moore is addressed in his private life. His wife calls him *Max* or *Darling* or *Sweetie Pie.* His children call him *Dad* or *Daddy* or *Father.* His nieces and nephews call him *Uncle Max.* His grandchildren will call him *Granddaddy, Granddad Max, Grandfather,* or *Grandfather Moore.* He has an old friend who addresses him as *Tiger,* and another who calls him *Buster.* All these must be capitalized if they are used to address a particular person or to speak of this particular person.

Family titles, terms of endearment, and nicknames are capitalized when they are used as names. They are not capitalized when they are used as common nouns that only show a type of person.

> Do you know, Darling, what time it is?
> That little girl is such a darling.

> Tell Father I will be back in a minute.
> Your father will pick you up from school.

> Uncle Max is our favorite uncle.

> I made this porcupine for you, Grandfather.
> Her grandfather lives a mile away.

> How has life been treating you, Tiger?
> He was a tiger on the football field.

EXERCISE 48: In every sentence, underline the first letter of any word that should be capitalized.

1. she said, "we came to see wendy williams."

2. as it happened, aunt wendy was out.

3. i told her, "mayor williams is at the town hall."

4. my aunt was elected the mayor of foxville a year ago.

5. before her, captain brassbound had been our mayor.

6. he used to say, "we'll get this town shipshape yet."

7. brassbound had been a captain in the navy before he settled in wisconsin.

8. as soon as he saw foxville, he said, "that's the place for me."

9. his wife is judge brassbound of the federal district court.

10. my mother is doctor alexandra malone.

11. at times, dad calls her alex or sandy or santa.

12. her old patients call her doctor alexandra.

13. she became a doctor before i was born.

14. when mom was born, granddad was a professor.

15. he told me that she was a very cheerful infant.

16. people would say, "oh, professor, what a bright baby you have!"

17. now people say to her, "oh, doctor, what a famous father you have!"

18. my grandfather has been a senator for three years.

19. sometimes i call him senator robinson.

20. i also like to address my aunt as madam mayor.

Geographic Names

Capitalize any part of the world that has a name of its own. Capitalize it whether it is large or small, dry or wet, natural or man-made, provided it has a name of its own.

If the article *the* precedes the name, don't capitalize the article unless it begins the sentence.

A name that consists of two words or more will often contain one word that can also be used as a common noun. That noun is capitalized as part of the name, but not when used as a common noun.

the Milky Way	the way, the galaxy
Aquarius	the constellation
Mars	the planet
the Northern Hemisphere	a hemisphere
the South Pole	south of here
the Pacific Ocean	the ocean
the Ohio River	the river
Lake Superior	the lake
the Bay of Mexico	the bay
the Hawaiian Islands	the islands
the Olympic Peninsula	the peninsula
the Rocky Mountains	the mountains
Mount Everest	
the Sahara Desert	the desert
North America	a continent, north of here
Canada	the country
Ontario Province	the province
Texas	a state
the Lone Star State	the state of Texas
Orange County	the county
New York City	the city
Washington, D.C.	the city of Washington, the capital
Pennsylvania Avenue	the avenue
the White House	the house

the Empire State Building	the building
the Golden Gate Bridge	the bridge
St. Patrick's Cathedral	the cathedral
Mildred Millstone High School	the high school
Columbia College	the college
the Metropolitan Museum	the museum
the Palace Theater	the theater, a palace

EXERCISE 49: Underline the first letter of any word that should be capitalized.

1. one half of bear lake is in idaho, the other half in utah.
2. the lake is about twenty miles long.
3. five states have a mountain named bear mountain.
4. one is in san juan county, colorado.
5. another is in the town of salisbury, connecticut.
6. a third is on the hudson river in the state of new york.
7. near it is the bear mountain bridge, which spans the river.
8. the fourth and fifth are in pennsylvania and south dakota.
9. just south of new york city, the hudson flows into the atlantic ocean.
10. galveston is a city on the gulf of mexico.
11. it is situated to the southeast of houston, texas.
12. we will spend our vacation in the blue mountains, between the columbia river and the snake river.
13. i would like to see a desert in the southern hemisphere.
14. at one time, the sahara desert had vegetation and was not a desert.
15. i would rather go to the north pole than to mars.
16. my uncle has an apartment in the lincoln building.
17. the building is one block south of lincoln square.
18. that square is the largest in the city of foxville.
19. foxville college is on its north side, and our museum is on its west side.
20. the greenleaf theater is at the back of the college, on crow street.

Names of Books, Newspapers, Magazines, Plays, Films, Musical Works, Art Works, Awards, Prizes, Firms, Trademarks, Organizations, Government Departments, Wars, Revolutions, Historic Documents, Historical Eras, Ships, Spacecraft

When you refer to any one of the items listed above by its actual name, capitalize it exactly as you capitalize non-sentences. That means: capitalize all parts of the name except the conjunctions *and, or,* the articles *an, a, the,* and prepositions of less than five letters, unless they begin or end the name.

BOOK: How to Win Friends and Influence People
NEWSPAPER: Washington Post
MAGAZINE: Better Homes and Gardens
PLAY: The Taming of the Shrew
FILM: Gone with the Wind
MUSICAL WORK: Symphony No. 1 in C Major
ART WORK: Night View of Toledo
AWARD: Congressional Medal of Honor
PRIZE: Nobel Prize for Medicine
FIRM: John J. Moneymaker and Sons
TRADEMARK: Chevrolet
ORGANIZATION: American Society for the Prevention of Cruelty to Animals (ASPCA)
GOVERNMENT DEPARTMENT: Department of Labor
WAR: Vietnam War
REVOLUTION: French Revolution
HISTORIC DOCUMENT: the U.S. Constitution
HISTORICAL ERA: Middle Ages
SHIP: Queen of the Caribbean
SPACECRAFT: Voyager II

EXERCISE 50: Underline the first letter of any word that should be capitalized.

1. did you hear our performance of handel's messiah?

2. the declaration of independence was adopted in 1776.

3. we read samuel butler's novel, the way of all flesh.

4. this car was made by the chrysler corporation.

5. bob has joined the boy scouts of america.

6. robert duvall won an oscar for his performance in the film called tender mercies.

7. edgar hoover directed the federal bureau of investigation (FBI).

8. during the ice age, glaciers covered all of canada.

9. do you believe all you read in the national enquirer?

10. i'm going out to buy quaker oats.

Religions, Their Adherents, Their Adjectives

Capitalize all religions, their adherents, and the adjectives derived from them.

Christianity	Christians	Christian beliefs
Catholicism	Catholics	Catholic beliefs
Protestantism	Protestants	Protestant beliefs
Judaism	Jews	Jewish beliefs
Islam	Muslims	Muslim beliefs
Buddhism	Buddhists	Buddhist beliefs

Capitalize all religious sects, their adherents, and their adjectives.

Puritanism	Puritan(s)
Christian Science	Christian Scientist(s)
Fundamentalism	Fundamentalist(s)
	Baptist(s)
	Shi'ite Muslims
	Zen Buddhist(s)

When referring to those worshipped in Christian or Jewish religion, the following are treated like names and are always capitalized.

God	Christ	the Holy Spirit
the Almighty	the Messiah	the Madonna
the Omnipotent	the Savior	the Virgin

Most of the preceding words can also be used in other contexts, and then they are not capitalized.

Zeus was the god of thunder.
The emperor was omnipotent.
This horse has a lot of spirit.
The priestesses of the goddess had to be virgins.

Politics, Nationality, Local Origins

Capitalize the name of a political party and anyone who belongs to it.

Democratic Party   a registered Democrat
Republican Party   a registered Republican
Communist Party   a card-carrying Communist

The adjectives *democratic, republican, communist* are not capitalized unless they mean "belonging to the Democratic Party, the Republican Party, or the Communist Party."

the Democratic senator
Republican economic policy
the Communist candidate

Do not capitalize a form of government, such as *democracy, communism, socialism, fascism, imperialism*.

Just as the names of continents, countries, states, and cities are capitalized, so are the particular nouns and adjectives that refer to them.

Europe—European(s)   France—(the) French
Africa—African(s)   Switzerland—(the) Swiss
Asia—Asian(s)   Holland—(the) Dutch
America—American(s)   Italy—Italian(s)

Texas—Texan(s)   Boston—Bostonian(s)
Georgia—Georgian(s)   Paris—Parisian(s)

EXCEPTIONS

With some expressions, everybody has long forgotten that they contain a word which refers to a country or city. In such cases, the word is not capitalized, though we would capitalize it in all other contexts. Take *french fries* as an example. That word combination has almost become one word, and no one thinks of the fact that, ages ago, we must have learned this way of preparing potatoes from the French. Furthermore, *french* is not really functioning as a nationality in this combination. We don't have the choice of ordering *Mexican* or *Hungarian* fries instead.

Other words or word combinations in which we no longer capitalize local or national origin include the following.

arabic numerals   brussels sprouts
china (porcelain)   danish pastries
bohemian (way of life)   dutch oven

frankfurters	plaster of paris
french dressing	portland cement
french fries	roman numerals
french windows	russian dressing
hamburgers	scotch whiskey
italics	turkish towels
manila envelopes	venetian blinds
morocco leather	

The Calendar

Capitalize the names of the months, of the days of the week, and of religious or national holidays.

> We celebrated Mother's Day on Sunday, May 13, and Halloween on October 31.

> I made my Halloween costume on Monday, October 8, which was Columbus Day in the United States and Thanksgiving Day in Canada.

> The dates of Christmas and New Year's Eve never vary, but the dates of Good Friday, Easter, and Passover do.

Words like *day, month, season, spring, summer, holiday, year,* or *century* are not names. They are common nouns and are therefore not capitalized when they stand on their own.

EXERCISE 51: Underline the first letter of any word that should be capitalized.

1. my birthday is on may 24, which used to be a national holiday in england.

2. for americans, thanksgiving day is the fourth thursday in november; for canadians, it is the second monday in october.

3. the christian holiday easter is celebrated on the sunday that follows the first full moon in spring.

4. one french friend and two texans i met in an italian museum will visit me on father's day.

5. the following day they hope to meet the republican governor of our state.

6. in some european democracies, such as france and italy, the communist party is quite large, but in most of them, socialism is more popular than communism.

7. in the arabic countries of africa, most people are neither jews nor christians, but muslims.

8. most swedish and norwegian people are protestants, as are the dutch.

9. the puritans were english protestants who had embarked on the mayflower to sail to virginia but arrived in massachusetts.

10. in the fall of 1621, those who had survived the harsh northern winter held a ceremony to thank god, and so started the north american tradition of celebrating thanksgiving day.

For additional practice, turn to the review test for this chapter at the back of the book.

6. WORDS TO CHECK

In this section you will find lists of irregular plurals and an alphabetical list of irregular verbs.

NOUNS WITH IRREGULAR PLURALS

In French and English, the "regular" way of forming the plural of a noun is to add -s to its singular form. Most languages form their noun plurals in much more complicated ways, and so did the old language of England, Anglo-Saxon. Then in 1066 A.D., the French-speaking Normans conquered England and ruled it for several centuries. In the course of those centuries, hundreds of French words drifted into the language of England, and so did the French method of forming plurals by adding -s. What had been Anglo-Saxon, or Old English, became Middle English, and then modern English.

In modern English, we still have some Anglo-Saxon plurals. They are the plurals of nouns that were so commonly used at the time of the Normans that they resisted the newfangled French way of forming the plural by adding an s.

man—men	mouse—mice
woman—women	goose—geese
child—children	tooth—teeth
ox—oxen	foot—feet

The following nouns are irregular in that their plural form is the same as their singular form.

deer—deer	fish—fish
sheep—sheep	shrimp—shrimp

110

Greek and Latin Nouns

Some English nouns with irregular plurals have come from a foreign language and form their plurals exactly as they are formed in the foreign language. Unlike the Anglo-Saxon words, which are everyday words, these borrowed words are scholarly words and mostly identify abstract ideas.

FROM GREEK	FROM LATIN
basis—bases	appendix—appendices
crisis—crises	index—indices
thesis—theses	alumnus—alumni
parenthesis—parentheses	alumna—alumnae
hypothesis—hypotheses	larva—larvae
antithesis—antitheses	vertebra—vertebrae
phenomenon—phenomena	bacterium—bacteria
criterion—criteria	ovum—ova
	datum—data
	medium—media

In English, these plurals are irregular because they don't add -s or -es to the singular form, but they are quite regular in the languages of their origin.

You can see that in Greek a singular ending in -is becomes a plural ending in -es; that a singular ending in -on becomes a plural ending in -a.

You can see that in Latin a singular ending in -x becomes a plural ending in -ces; a singular ending in -us becomes a plural ending in -i; a singular ending in -a becomes a plural ending in -ae; and a singular ending in -um becomes a plural ending in -a.

With these nouns from Greek and Latin, a lot of people don't know whether they're using the singular form or the plural.

Look through both lists and put a checkmark beside any word you might use yourself. Then learn the singular and the plural of each, and know which is which. Why should you? So that you can use them correctly. So that you don't use a singular verb form with a plural noun.

IRREGULAR VERBS

When we speak of *regular verbs* and *irregular verbs,* we don't mean good little verbs and naughty verbs. We mean verbs that do or don't form their simple past and past participle by adding -ed or -d to their plain form.

If you have read the preceding section on irregular noun plurals, you will guess correctly that the verbs of French origin are regular and form their simple past and past participle with -ed or -d. You will also guess that the irregular verbs are old Anglo-Saxon verbs.

Some Anglo-Saxon verbs became regular verbs in the course of time (*wash–washed–washed, flow–flowed–flowed*). Some Anglo-Saxon verbs now have the same irregular form for the simple past and the past participle (*buy–bought–bought, think–thought–thought*).

A third type of Anglo-Saxon verb is totally irregular, with three different forms for its three principal parts (*begin–began–begun, forbid–forbade–forbidden*). With this type, people make mistakes in the passive voice and in verb phrases made with *has, have,* or *had,* which must all be used with the past participle. Sometimes they are used with the simple past by people who don't know their grammar. It is wrong to say *he was shook, she has forgot, we had rode.* The correct forms are *he was shaken, she has forgotten, we had ridden.*

The other irregular verbs listed here are those that don't change at all from plain form to simple past to past participle. With these verbs, as with all other irregular verbs, it is a mistake to add -ed to them in the simple past or the past participle.

The Principal Parts of Irregular Verbs

PLAIN FORM	SIMPLE PAST	PAST PARTICIPLE
bear	bore	born, borne
beat	beat	beaten
become	became	become
begin	began	begun
bend	bent	bent
bet	bet	bet
bid	bade	bidden
bite	bit	bitten
blow	blew	blown
break	broke	broken
build	built	built
burst	burst	burst
buy	bought	bought
cast	cast	cast
catch	caught	caught
choose	chose	chosen
come	came	come
cost	cost	cost

PLAIN FORM	SIMPLE PAST	PAST PARTICIPLE
creep	crept	crept
cut	cut	cut
deal	dealt	dealt
dig	dug	dug
do	did	done
draw	drew	drawn
drink	drank	drunk
drive	drove	driven
eat	ate	eaten
fall	fell	fallen
feed	fed	fed
feel	felt	felt
fight	fought	fought
find	found	found
flee	fled	fled
fling	flung	flung
fly	flew	flown
forbid	forbade	forbidden
forget	forgot	forgotten
forgive	forgave	forgiven
freeze	froze	frozen
get	got	got, gotten
give	gave	given
go	went	gone
grind	ground	ground
grow	grew	grown
hang	hung	hung
have	had	had
hear	heard	heard
hide	hid	hidden
hit	hit	hit
hold	held	held
hurt	hurt	hurt
kneel	knelt	knelt
know	knew	known
lay	laid	laid
lead	led	led
leave	left	left
lend	lent	lent
let	let	let
lie	lay	lain
light	lit	lit

PLAIN FORM	SIMPLE PAST	PAST PARTICIPLE
lose	lost	lost
make	made	made
meet	met	met
mistake	mistook	mistaken
pay	paid	paid
put	put	put
quit	quit	quit
ride	rode	ridden
ring	rang	rung
rise	rose	risen
run	ran	run
say	said	said
see	saw	seen
seek	sought	sought
sell	sold	sold
send	sent	sent
set	set	set
shake	shook	shaken
shine	shone	shone
shoot	shot	shot
shrink	shrank	shrunk
shut	shut	shut
sing	sang	sung
sink	sank	sunk
sit	sat	sat
slay	slew	slain
sleep	slept	slept
slide	slid	slid
sling	slung	slung
speak	spoke	spoken
spend	spent	spent
spin	spun	spun
spit	spat	spat
split	split	split
spread	spread	spread
spring	sprang	sprung
stand	stood	stood
steal	stole	stolen
stick	stuck	stuck
sting	stung	stung
stink	stank	stunk

PLAIN FORM	SIMPLE PAST	PAST PARTICIPLE
strike	struck	struck
string	strung	strung
swear	swore	sworn
sweep	swept	swept
swim	swam	swum
swing	swung	swung
take	took	taken
teach	taught	taught
tear	tore	torn
think	thought	thought
throw	threw	thrown
wake	woke	woken
wear	wore	worn
weave	wove	woven
weep	wept	wept
win	won	won
wind	wound	wound
wring	wrang	wrung
write	wrote	written

7. MASTERY TESTS

PRETEST

The following six-section test has been designed to help you assess which chapters of this book you need to study most carefully. Take as much time as you need to work through the entire test, and then check your answers. By filling out the chart at the end of the test, you will be able to identify which points of grammar are problems for you and which pages in this book will help you resolve those problems. The test will also tell you which points of grammar are *not* problems for you and thus which parts of this book you need only review.

Section 1

Part A: Underline the incorrectly spelled nouns in these sentences. Rewrite the words correctly in the answer blanks.

1. I hate taking surprise quizes in this class. _____

2. The union questioned the company's vacation policys and demanded more holidaies for its members. _____

3. Native American tribes often hunted deers and caught fishes. _____

4. I tried to look up Mary Haggarty, but there were six Mary Haggarties in the phone book. _____

5. Lady and gentlemans, I am your host for the evening. _____

6. One of my favorite playes is *The Little Foxs*. _____

7. I bought some shrimps for dinner. _____

Part B: In each sentence, choose the correct noun form.

8. (Bobs and Dots/Bob's and Dot's/Bob and Dot's) _____ car was stolen last night.

9. I love that (actress/actress's/actress') _____ wardrobe.

10. The (womans/women's/womens') _____ department is on the third floor.

11. Both sets of (grandparents/grandparent's/grandparents')

    _____ spoil him horribly.

12. All of the (bosses/boss's/bosses') _____ offices, along

    with the (employees/employee's/employees') _____ cafeteria, were repainted over the weekend.

13. The conference dealt with (Lebanon and Israel/Lebanon's and Israel's/Lebanon and Israel's) _____ shared border.

14. Is a (wasps/wasp's/wasps') _____ sting worse than a

    (bees/bee's/bees') _____?

Part C: Underline the first letter of any word that should be capitalized.

15. followers of islam are called muslims.

16. a galaxy is composed of gas, dust, and stars.

17. we went to a fourth of july picnic.

18. thank god, you're safe!

19. our streets, mr. mayor, are full of potholes.

20. we ate the best french fries in iowa city.

21. may i borrow the car, dad?

22. over the summer, i plan to read *war and peace*.

23. is reverend barkley a lutheran minister?

24. the verrazano-narrows bridge is the longest suspension bridge in the u.s.

25. we built the cottage on the northern shore of the lake.

26. do any doctors make house calls?

27. does doctor bruno have evening office hours?

28. the democratic party has 45 senators this term.

29. i like watching television on thursday nights.

30. the british government called for an end to the coal strike.

31. i broke one of my grandmother's china teacups.

32. pennsylvania is known as the keystone state.

33. what are the major principles of socialism?

34. we watched the buddhist priests conduct the ceremony at the temple.

35. the civil aeronautics board will announce its findings tomorrow.

Section 2

Part A: In each sentence, use the appropriate form of the verb in parentheses.

1. During the storm, our dog had _____ under the porch. (hide)

2. My parents were _____ $55,000 for their house. (offer)

3. The next time you see me, I will have _____ a beard. (grow)

4. She was _____ her memoirs when she died. (write)

5. They are _____ to move this weekend. (plan)

6. The prisoner was _____ in solitary confinement. (put)

7. The guerillas were _____ cars and trucks from entering the town. (stop)

8. I've _____ my children to be independent. (teach)

9. By tonight, we will have _____ 550 miles. (drive)

10. "I haven't _____ moody," he said crossly. (be)

11. Andrea will be _____ a surprise birthday party for Peter tomorrow. (throw)

12. Climbing over the rocks, he had _____ out his sneakers. (wear)

Part B: Underline any incorrect verb form, and write the correct form in the blank. If a sentence contains no error, write "correct" in the blank.

_____ 13. Georgetown has beat St. John's for the championship.

_____ 14. Following the accident, the traffic grinded to a halt.

_____ 15. If I were ugly, would you still love me?

_____ 16. The treasure was hid under the floorboards.

_____ 17. Were'nt they upset that you were late?

_____ 18. You couldn't have drank the whole bottle by yourself!

_____ 19. Have you ever rode a horse?

_____ 20. If I was a millionaire, I'd own a yacht.

_____ 21. I have'nt been feeling well lately.

_____ 22. After the game, I lied down for a nap.

_____ 23. He had broken all of his promises to me.

_____ 24. The jury was showed the incriminating evidence.

_____ 25. I think the geese may have flew south already.

_____ 26. I recommend that he is given parole.

Section 3

Choose the correct verb form in each sentence.

1. (Doesn't/Don't) _____ George and Jackie own a car?

2. The books (was/were) _____ printed in Yiddish.

3. My grades on this report card (was/were) _____ better than I had expected.

4. Her children (is/are) _____ her only comfort.

5. What (is/are) _____ the arrangements for Wednesday?

6. There (is/are) _____ four people waiting to use the tennis courts.

7. Nothing ever (seem/seems) _____ to bother him.

8. Both of the candidates (has/have) _____ made wild accusations.

9. Katharine Hepburn and Humphrey Bogart (star/stars)

   _____ in *The African Queen*.

10. Either the dentist or his assistant (clean/cleans) _____ my teeth.

11. She (does/do) _____ the laundry when she comes home from work.

12. The crew (was/were) _____ studying their navigation plans.

13. Half of the crop (was/were) _____ destroyed by the frost.

14. News (is/are) _____ censored in many countries.

15. (Was/Were) _____ your brother and sister at home?

16. The union (has/have) _____ sided with the mechanics in the strike.

17. (Does/Do) _____ the Detroit Tigers have a game tomorrow?

18. The model with defective brakes (has/have) _____ been recalled by the company.

19. The cause of his headaches (is/are) _____ still unknown.

20. Which one of these sweaters (belong/belongs) _____ to Pat?

21. Here (come/comes) _____ the President's motorcade.

22. (Is/Are) _____ there any messages for me?

23. Some of the miners (was/were) _____ injured in the explosion.

24. Her son or her daughter (is/are) _____ going to accompany her.

25. Neither the state nor the federal government (has/have) _____ enough money for this fiscal year.

26. The crowd (is/are) _____ growing impatient.

27. Most of the people in that country (was/were) _____ starving.

28. Ethics (is/are) _____ the study of moral values.

29. The laws of physics (is/are) _____ difficult to understand.

30. The craters of the moon (doesn't/don't) _____ appear to shelter any forms of life.

31. Columbus, as well as other captains, (was/were) _____ looking for a sea route from Europe to India.

32. (Is/Are) _____ the sleeves of this jacket too long for me?

33. Reactions to the President's proposed budget (is/are) _____ likely to be unfavorable.

34. (Has/Have) _____ the council passed this resolution?

35. Oatmeal and milk (is/are) _____ a filling breakfast.

36. The meal together with tip (come/comes) _____ to $14.95.

37. The largest of the three cars (belong/belongs) _____ to my sister.

38. There (was/were) _____ times when I regretted my decision.

39. The plan of the generals (was/were) _____ to attack the enemy from the rear.

40. The mayor, accompanied by two of his deputies, (is/are) _____ going to arrive at 8 o'clock.

Section 4

In each sentence, choose the correct pronoun form.

1. (Us/We) _____ and (them/they) _____ met at the bus stop.

2. Can (him/he) _____ and his wife come for dinner?

3. Terry told Linda and (us/we) _____ that you won the lottery.

4. The judge gave (him/he) _____ and his accomplice a heavy sentence.

5. Between you and (me/I) _____, I think she's lying.

6. To (us/we) _____, the fire seemed to be coming in our direction.

7. "It was (me/I) _____ who killed Mrs. Godfrey," he whispered fiendishly.

8. Are you implying that it was (her/she) _____ who committed the crime?

9. Rich people are not like (we/us) _____; they have money.

10. My son is already as tall as (me/I) _____.

11. They invited Harry and (me/myself) _____ to a Halloween party.

12. Christine and (I/myself) _____ want to thank you for your gift.

13. The guests can help (themselves/theirselves) _____ to the appetizers.

14. I bought (me/myself) _____ a new motorcycle.

15. He (hisself/himself) _____ said the speech was too long.

16. I don't think (theirs/their) _____ suggestion is very practical.

17. I don't think their idea is as good as (ours/our's) _____.

18. That red Corvette is (mine/mines) _____.

19. The Chinese often eat soup after (there/their/they're) _____ main course.

20. (Your/You're) _____ coming today was a big surprise.

21. (Its/It's) _____ not the first time you've been wrong.

22. (Their/There's) _____ is not an easy life.

23. (Those were/That was) _____ the good old days.

24. (These are/This is) _____ one of the happiest days of my life.

25. (These here/These) _____ are my cousins, Floyd and Betty Lou.

26. Give me (those/them) _____ lamb chops over there.

27. There was (this/a) _____ weird woman on the train this morning.

28. A person (who/that) _____ gets angry easily may have few friends.

29. Running, (which/that) _____ is my favorite form of exercise, relaxes me after a long day of working.

30. (Whose/Who's) _____ able to say what the future holds?

31. I'm sure it was Maurice (who/whom) _____ tried to call me last night.

32. To (who/whom) _____ should I make out this check?

33. (Who/Whom) _____ do you think will win the fight?

34. It was we (who/whom) _____ organized the rally.

35. The letter was addressed "To (who/whom) _____ it may concern."

36. Bruce Springsteen is a songwriter (who/whom) _____ people are beginning to appreciate.

37. I didn't see (anything/nothing) _____ wrong with that answer.

38. Doesn't (anyone/no one) _____ have the right time?

Section 5

Part A: Choose the correct article, adjective, or adverb form in each of these sentences.

1. I want to grow (a/an) _____ herb garden this summer.

2. Have you ever seen (a/an) _____ unicorn?

3. We watched (a/an) _____ eagle soar majestically over the forest.

4. Scrooge (greedyly/greedily) _____ counted his money.

5. She (actively/activly) _____ campaigned for Jackson.

6. I (accidentally/accidently) _____ knocked over your crystal vase.

7. His singing sounded (horrible/horribly) _____.

8. They looked (questioning/questioningly) _____ at me.

9. That was (awful/awfully) _____ kind of you.

10. She seemed very (serious/seriously) _____.

11. They sounded the alarm (quick/quickly) _____.

12. That was a (real/really) _____ close call!

13. Despite his illness, he remains (happy/happily) _____.

14. She looked (angry/angrily) _____ at the past-due bill.

Part B: Find the comparison mistakes in these sentences. Rewrite the sentences correctly. There is one correct sentence.

15. His blood pressure is more high than it should be.

    _____

16. She was the extravagantest person I ever knew.

    _____

17. Cocker spaniels are friendliest than bulldogs.

    _____

18. Carl Lewis jumped more far than the other athletes.

    _____

19. Bob drives too fastly.

    _____

20. Which volcano has erupted recentest?

    _____

21. The last letter that John wrote was the longest of all.

_____

22. Few substances are more cheap.

_____

23. The team practices more harder than ever.

_____

24. Is wool the durablest fabric?

_____

25. You're least excited about the trip than I am.

_____

26. He drives even more fast than you do.

_____

27. This tastes gooder than I thought it would.

_____

28. Donna dresses elegantest.

_____

29. Jim's cooking is even worst than mine.

_____

30. I had the most horriblest dream last night.

_____

31. Do lions run fastest than cheetahs?

_____

32. This is the worse movie I've ever seen.

_____

33. The king cobra is the longer species of snake.

_____

34. Of the three candidates, Fenwick is less likely to win.

_____

Section 6

Part A: Some of the sentences below are complete, some are incomplete. Rewrite a complete sentence using capital letter(s) and correct end mark. If the sentence is not complete, write "incomplete sentence" in the blank.

1. over two hundred years ago

   _____

2. she asked me if we wanted to come

   _____

3. at last i've found you

   _____

4. everyone thought the decision was fair

   _____

5. although he's almost 94 years old

   _____

6. shouldn't you be going to work

   _____

7. send me a postcard when you get there

   _____

8. among the six of them, they planned the escapade

   _____

9. as long as it's not too hot

   _____

10. which recipe do you like the best

   _____

Part B: Assume that each of the following lines is a heading or title. Underline the first letter of every word that should be capitalized.

11. you're nice to be with

12. me and you against the world

13. people—and other strange animals

14. incredible but true

15. hair: a musical

In this chart, find the number of any item that you did not answer correctly. The right-hand side of the chart will tell you the pages to study if you missed more than one item in a given group.

If you missed item number	Study the following pages
Section 1 1 2 3 4 5 6 7	Chapter 1, page 2; Chapter 6, pages 110–111
8 9 10 11 12 13 14	Chapter 5, pages 94–96
15 16 17 18 19 20 21 22 23 24 25 26 27 28 29 30 31 32 33 34 35	Chapter 1, pages 1–3; Chapter 5, pages 100–109
Section 2 1 2 3 4 5 6 7 8 9 10 11 12	Chapter 1, pages 6–13; Chapter 4, pages 69–70; Chapter 6, pages 112–115
13 14 15 16 17 18 19 20 21 22 23 24 25 26	Chapter 1, pages 6–12; Chapter 4, pages 69–74; Chapter 5, pages 89–91
Section 3 1 2 3 4 5 6 7 8 9 10 11 12 13 14 15 16 17 18 19 20 21 22 23 24 25 26 27 28 29 30 31 32 33 34 35 36 37 38 39 40	Chapter 2, pages 32–38; Chapter 3, pages 49–50; Chapter 4, pages 52–60

Section 4 1 2 3 4 5 6 7 8 9 10 11 12 13 14 15 16 17 18 19 20 21 22 23 24 25 26 27 28 29 30 31 32 33 34 35 36 37 38	Chapter 1, pages 21–26; Chapter 2, pages 38–43; Chapter 4, pages 61–67 & 84; Chapter 5, pages 92– 93
Section 5 1 2 3 4 5 6 7 8 9 10 11 12 13 14	Chapter 1, pages 14–21; Chapter 2, pages 44–45;
15 16 17 18 19 20 21 22 23 24 25 26 27 28 29 30 31 32 33 34	Chapter 4, pages 85–88; Chapter 4, pages 75–83
Section 6 1 2 3 4 5 6 7 8 9 10	Chapter 3, pages 46–51;
11 12 13 14 15	Chapter 5, pages 97–99

REVIEW TEST—CHAPTER 1.   PARTS OF SPEECH

Part A: Underline the capitalization and spelling mistakes in these sentences. Write the corrections in the answer blanks. A sentence may have more than one mistake in it.

1.   Matt drove from philadelphia to erie in eight hours.

_____

2.   He lived in germany for three Years.

_____

3.   We took two busses to get to the Hospital.

_____

4.   Taxs in this City are too high.

_____

5. Jane bought extra supplys for the camping trip.

   _____

6. Never walk down dark alleies.

   _____

7. Is february the coldest Month of the year?

   _____

8. I made some tuna sandwichs for lunch.

   _____

9. The sears tower is the tallest building in the World.

   _____

10. My Uncle will be staying at the holiday inn.

Part B: Underline the verb phrase (all action, linking, and helping verbs, as well as any modals) in each of these sentences.

11. Her father had been ill for many years.
12. Who has won the lottery?
13. Jim should have called earlier.
14. Did you pay the electric bill?
15. I will be leaving tomorrow.
16. Frank may bowl with us on Tuesday.
17. Karen might have taken a wrong turn.
18. The Johnsons are moving in March.
19. The country will elect a new prime minister next year.
20. Can you imitate Humphrey Bogart?
21. David has been running since his college days.
22. I must do the dishes.
23. The driver was given a sobriety test.
24. Chocolate will be my downfall.

25. A relief pitcher was throwing in the bull pen.

In each sentence, use the appropriate form of the verb in parentheses. Use either the present participle or the past participle.

26. We have _____ our stay at this hotel. (enjoy)

27. The celebrity was _____ the key to the city. (give)

28. By the time you see me, I will have _____ ten pounds. (lose)

29. She was _____ throughout the movie. (cry)

30. I had _____ what day it was. (forget)

31. Lester has _____ a beard. (grow)

32. You're _____ on my foot! (step)

33. Has she _____ her promise? (break)

34. The toddler was _____ a tantrum. (throw)

35. He was _____ to have a bad temper. (know)

36. The audience was _____ enthusiastically. (clap)

37. I had _____ to be finished by now. (hope)

38. They will have _____ dinner before we get there. (eat)

39. Lisa was _____ over the speed limit when the accident occurred. (drive)

40. I've _____ that movie before. (see)

41. The wind had _____ down the power lines. (blow)

42. I'm sure he will have _____ reservations for us. (make)

43. I'm _____ to return to school. (plan)

44. The robber was _____ with the stolen jewelry on him. (catch)

45. The prisoner was _____ to make one phone call. (allow)

46. Are you _____ in the marathon this weekend? (run)

47. She said he had _____ a good job. (find)

48. By the end of this vacation, I will have _____ sixty pictures. (take)

49. The package was _____ to the wrong address. (send)

Part C: In each sentence, indicate whether the word in italics is functioning as an adjective (A), a noun (N), or a verb (V).

_____ **50.** someone is *following* us.

_____ **51.** Read the *following* directions carefully.

_____ **52.** This *show* is a rerun.

_____ **53.** I lost a pair of *gold* earrings.

_____ **54.** He always eats two *fried* eggs for breakfast.

_____ **55.** He *fried* two eggs for breakfast.

_____ **56.** Mother Teresa serves the *poor* of India.

_____ **57.** The *invited* guests arrived promptly at eight o'clock.

_____ **58.** I am taking a *singing* class.

_____ **59.** I am always *singing* in the shower.

_____ **60.** You are really being *stubborn* about this problem.

_____ **61.** The *football* players are entering the stadium.

_____ **62.** Jaworski threw the *football* eighty yards.

_____ **63.** We can learn much from the *past*.

_____ **64.** What did you do this *past* summer?

Write *a* or *an* before these words.

65. _____ American   **66.** _____ herb

67. _____ European   **68.** _____ history book

69. _____ utensil   **70.** _____ oyster

71. _____ usher   **72.** _____ euphoric feeling

73. _____ hour   **74.** _____ human being

Part D: Choose the correct word in each sentence.

75. The cat stretched (lazily/lazyly) in the sun.

76. This subway is (awful/awfully) slow.

77. Oscar is a (sloppy/sloppily) dresser.

78. I can't spell very (good/well).

79. This season the Orioles played (terrible/terribly).

80. She was parked (illegal/illegally) by a hydrant.

81. I (specifically/specificly) asked you for the exact change.

82. This stew smells (wonderful/wonderfully).

83. Maria didn't pass the test as (easyly/easily) as she thought she would.

84. He rearranged the files (systematic/systematically).

85. We had a (real/really) good time at the picnic.

86. The guard was (horribly/horribley) disfigured in the explosion.

87. The defendant gave a (convincing/convincingly) story to the jury.

88. "That didn't take you very long," he said (sarcasticly/sarcastically).

89. He's a (frequent/frequently) customer in this store.

90. You (great/greatly) exaggerated that story.

91. Just (simplely/simply) tell the truth.

92. You snore (loud/loudly).

93. You're a (loud/loudly) snorer.

94. (Basicly, Basically), we think alike.

95. She smiled at him (hopeful/hopefully).

96. The athletes were (intense/intensely).

Part E: Write the correct pronoun in each answer blank.

97. We bought (us/ourselves) _____ a new TV.

98. I pampered (myself/me) _____ with a bubble bath.

99. (Herself/She) _____ said it wouldn't work!

100. Tina and (myself/I) _____ were the first to arrive.

101. Cats always clean (itself/themselves) _____ after eating.

102. He walked (her/herself) _____ to her car.

103. The judge disqualified (himself/myself) _____ from the competition.

104. This present is for Jack and (you/yourself) _____.

105. The pitcher (who/that) _____ started yesterday has hurt his shoulder.

106. The statue (what/that) _____ we saw was very old.

107. This shirt, (which/what) _____ I bought on sale, is my favorite.

108. The waiter (who/which) _____ served us was Jennifer's brother.

109. Doesn't (nobody/everybody) _____ like the summer?

110. I haven't had (anything/nothing) _____ to eat yet today.

111. I told (no one/anyone) _____ about your plans.

112. (Something/Anything) _____ is wrong with the stereo.

113. Did (someone/anyone) _____ see my car keys?

114. She scarcely did (nothing/anything) _____ to bother him.

115. (Everybody/Anybody) _____ knows he's lying.

116. The boys said they didn't have (nothing/anything) _____ to do.

Part F: In each sentence, indicate whether the word(s) in italics is/are functioning as a preposition (P), conjunction (C), or interjection (I).

_____ **117.** *Ouch!* That hurt!

_____ **118.** Marci wasn't home *when* I called.

_____ **119.** He sat *behind* us at the concert.

—— **120.** She maneuvered the wheelchair *without* difficulty.

—— **121.** We skated *over* the frozen pond.

—— **122.** I washed the dishes *and* put them away.

—— **123.** Greg swam *in spite of* a cramp in his side.

—— **124.** *Oh, no!* I lost my pocket book!

—— **125.** You can stay here *as long as* you want.

—— **126.** I like to walk *in* the rain.

In this chart, find the number of any item that you did not answer correctly. The right-hand side of the chart will tell you the pages to review if you missed more than one item in a given group.

If you missed item numbers	Review the following pages
1 2 3 4 5 6 7 8 9 10	Chapter 1, pages 1–3
11 12 13 14 15 16 17 18 19 20 21 22 23 24 25 26 27 28 29 30 31 32 33 34 35 36 37 38 39 40 41 42 43 44 45 46 47 48 49	Chapter 1, pages 3–14
50 51 52 53 54 55 56 57 58 59 60 61 62 63 64 65 66 67 68 69 70 71 72 73 74	Chapter 1, pages 14–19
75 76 77 78 79 80 81 82 83 84 85 86 87 88 89 90 91 92 93 94 95 96	Chapter 1, pages 19–21
97 98 99 100 101 102 103 104 105 106 107 108 109 110 111 112 113 114 115 116	Chapter 1, pages 21–27
117 118 119 120 121 122 123 124 125 126	Chapter 1, pages 27–31

REVIEW TEST—CHAPTER 2.   PARTS OF THE SENTENCE

Part A: In each sentence, underline the simple subject. Then say on the answer line whether the subject is singular or plural, and in the first, second, or third person.

1. The Celtics and the Lakers played last night.

   _____

2. Upper Volta, a former French colony, changed its name to Bourkina Fasso.

   _____

3. Many evening students have full-time jobs.

   _____

4. I haven't had any heat in my apartment for a week.

   _____

5. That is Melissa's brother across the aisle.

   _____

6. Blue is my favorite color.

   _____

7. The mice in the cage seem frightened.

   _____

8. The trees that line our street are red maples.

   _____

9. You are awfully superstitious people.

   _____

10. She was the delegate elected to represent us.

   _____

11. Riding backwards on a train makes me nauseous.

   _____

12. They don't have a televison set.

   _____

13. This photograph of my grandparents was taken in 1910.

   _____

14. Swimming and biking are good forms of exercise.

   _____

15. Alexander, the king of Macedon, ruled a great empire.

   _____

16. The telephone number of my friend is unlisted.

   _____

17. A new department store and new office buildings are being developed.

   _____

18. We had to borrow money from the bank again.

   _____

19. These are troubled times.

   _____

20. You remind me of my brother.

   _____

21. The objects, round and glowing, sped through the dark sky.

   _____

22. Yellows are popular in fashion this year.

   _____

Part B: In each sentence, underline the simple subject. Then choose the verb form that agrees with the subject.

23. Rita and her husband (is/are) _____ planning a trip to Puerto Rico.

24. The hotel, modernized and redecorated, (has/have) _____ been attracting new guests.

25. Old, worn shoes (is/are) _____ usually more comfortable than new shoes.

26. Eating and sleeping (is/are) _____ the main interests of my cat.

27. I (has/have) _____ forgotten my keys again.

28. The bus, loaded with people, (was/were) _____ stalled in the parking lot.

29. The weak arguments of the prosecutor (has/have) _____ infuriated the judge.

30. You (was/were) _____ talking in your sleep again.

31. The sound of the drums (was/were) _____ deafening.

32. This (has/have) _____ been a long day.

33. The poor (has/have) _____ been hurt by the recession.

34. He (was/were) _____ shouting for no reason.

35. The roses which I bought yesterday (has/have) _____ withered.

36. Skiing down the slopes (was/were) _____ exhilarating.

37. You (has/have) _____ been trying too hard.

38. The brakes of this care (is/are) _____ not functioning properly.

39. My parents, who are retired, (has/have) _____ been doing volunteer work at the hospital.

40. Dogwoods and azaleas (was/were) _____ damaged by the frost.

41. We (was/were) _____ hoping to buy a new house.

42. Good (has/have) _____ triumphed over evil.

43. The squirrels in this tree (has/have) _____ been fighting for two hours.

44. My brother, David, (is/are) _____ moving to California.

Part C: In each sentence, identify the word(s) in *italics* as either a direct object (DO), an indirect object (IO), an object of a preposition (OP), or a subject complement (SC).

_____ 45. Darlene is wearing *an unusual-looking hat* today.

_____ 46. Steve gave *us* a souvenir from Mexico.

_____ **47.** It was *a futile gesture.*

_____ **48.** He bought a used van with *the prize money.*

_____ **49.** The mayor appointed *a new police commissioner* last week.

_____ **50.** I told him *the good news.*

_____ **51.** Setsuko taught *Kathleen* Japanese.

_____ **52.** Her story is *incredible.*

_____ **53.** Those books belong on *this shelf.*

_____ **54.** The restaurant caters *parties* and *weddings.*

_____ **55.** The best player on our team is *Larry.*

_____ **56.** My son gave *our dog* a bath.

_____ **57.** She went down *the stairs* slowly.

_____ **58.** Satellites are being used to explore the mysteries of *other planets.*

_____ **59.** Terry is *an experienced electrician.*

_____ **60.** Her singing is giving *me* a headache.

_____ **61.** The governor appeared *nervous* at his press conference.

_____ **62.** I sent a letter to *my representative.*

_____ **63.** I made Chris *a sandwich.*

_____ **64.** she gave *Pete* your phone number.

In this chart, find the number of any item that you did not answer correctly. The right-hand side of the chart will tell you the pages to review if you miss more than one item in a given group.

If you missed item number	Review the following pages
1 2 3 4 5 6 7 8 9 10 11 12 13 14 15 16 17 18 19 20 21 22	Chapter 2, pages 32–35
23 24 25 26 27 28 29 30 31 32 33 34 35 36 37 38 39 40 41 42 43 44	Chapter 2, pages 35–37

If you missed item number	Review the following pages
45 46 47 48 49 50 51 52 53 54 55 56 57 58 59 60 61 62 63 64	Chapter 2, pages 38–45

REVIEW TEST—CHAPTER 3.   SENTENCE TYPES

Part A: Some of the following sentences are complete, and some are incomplete. Mark a complete sentence with a **C** in the answer blank. For an incomplete sentence, use the answer blank to say what the sentence needs. Use **SC** for subject complement, **DO** for direct object, or **IC** for independent clause.

_____ 1.   For their anniversary, Eric gave Alicia.

_____ 2.   After you left the party.

_____ 3.   Yesterday I worked out at the gym.

_____ 4.   If the water shortage continues.

_____ 5.   The expensive candy that we bought was.

_____ 6.   The suitcase was heavier than I expected.

_____ 7.   One of the foremost architects in the nation designed.

_____ 8.   Once you have learned to ride a bike.

_____ 9.   Their lawn looks.

_____ 10.   Having won the election by a huge margin.

Part B: First, add the missing end punctuation to each sentence below. Next, tell what type of sentence it is. Label the sentence **D** for declarative sentence, **Q** for question, **I** for imperative sentence, or **E** for exclamatory sentence.

_____ 11.   Hurricane Hazel is headed straight for Miami

_____ 12. Bert needs to know how Josef spells his last name

_____ 13. Close the door after you leave

_____ 14. The directions on the package must be followed exactly

_____ 15. Shouldn't we be leaving now

_____ 16. How I wish I could go

_____ 17. Watch the signs as you approach the cut-off

_____ 18. Let's get out of here

_____ 19. He asked if you had eaten dinner yet

_____ 20. Whom did he want to see

Part C: Rewrite the following sentences in question form.

21. He drove all the way to Washington in one day.

_____

22. The mechanic can't find the problem with the transmission.

_____

23. Calvin has been in a car accident.

_____

24. The infant was sleeping when the phone rang.

_____

25. The twins catch colds very easily.

_____

26. Ralph and Ed have filed for unemployment.

_____

27. The Braggs are hoping to qualify for the loan.

_____

28. That building had been inspected just before the fire.

_____

29. The tiger cub is very tame.

_____

30. Cynthia will be bringing the wine.

_____

31. We should call the police.

_____

32. Jose will have finished dinner by seven o'clock.

_____

33. The passengers survived the crash.

_____

34. Lucy isn't going to her exercise class.

_____

35. The rain had ruined the parade.

_____

36. The fans were shouting at the referee.

_____

37. Maria worries about everything.

_____

38. Joyce and Ben went to Barbados for their vacation.

_____

In this chart, find the number of any item that you did not answer correctly. The right-hand side of the chart will tell you the pages to review if you missed more than one item in a given group.

If you missed item number	Review the following pages
1 2 3 4 5 6 7 8 9 10	Chapter 3, pages 46–48
11 12 13 14 15 16 17 18 19 20	Chapter 3, pages 46–51
21 22 23 24 25 26 27 28 29 30 31 32 33 34 35 36 37 38	Chapter 3, pages 48–50

REVIEW TEST—CHAPTER 4. USING THE PARTS OF SPEECH CORRECTLY

Part A: Choose the correct verb form in each sentence.

1. (Don't/Doesn't) _____ you want us to wait for you?

2. One of the books (is/are) _____ overdue.

3. The clerk (was/were) _____ very rude to us.

4. The two countries (has/have) _____ agreed to a ceasefire.

5. That outfit of hers (look/looks) _____ terrible.

6. The people Frank invited (is/are) _____ from Canada.

7. The council (has/have) _____ withdrawn its support for the bill.

8. Measles (is/are) _____ a potentially dangerous disease.

9. We (do/does) _____ crossword puzzles together.

10. The woolen and acrylic sweaters on the third floor (is/are) _____ on sale.

11. Chocolate chip cookies (is/are) _____ my weakness.

12. There (was/were) _____ three people injured in the crash.

13. No one (get/gets) _____ in without paying admission.

14. Natural gas and coal (is/are) _____ safe sources of energy.

15. Geometry as well as chemistry (was/were) _____ difficult for me to understand.

16. Why (has/have) _____ the site of the protests been changed?

17. Every man and woman (has/have) _____ the right to be free.

18. This crew (work/works) _____ well.

19. (Do/Does) _____ the cashier have change for a dollar?

20. Neither Brad nor Carl (has/have) _____ been offered the job.

21. Here (lie/lies) _____ John Doe and his wife.

22. Her intelligence, along with her charm, (impress/impresses) _____ him.

23. My confidant and best friend (is/are) _____ my husband.

24. The cause of the hives (was/were) _____ allergic reactions to peanuts and MSG.

25. Many (is/are) _____ called; few chosen.

26. Either my mother or my father (is/are) _____ going with me.

27. His ideas (don't/doesn't) _____ seem very practical.

28. The team (require/requires) _____ extra-large uniforms.

29. Most of the crowd (has/have) _____ left already.

30. He (has/have) _____ an extremely large nose.

31. His only habit (was/were) _____ cigarettes.

32. Half of the tomatoes (was/were) _____ rotten.

33. Employment applications for the summer job program (is/are) _____ available now.

34. Where in the attic (is/are) _____ the old costumes stored?

35. Several of the signatures (was/were) _____ found to be forged.

36. Molasses (is/are) _____ the secret ingredient in this recipe.

Part B: In each sentence, choose the correct pronoun form.

37. Oscar and (me/I) _____ went to the racetrack.

38. You are as tall as (him/he) _____.

39. They have hurt (themselves/theirselves) _____ again.

40. That award was (her/hers) _____.

41. The conductor told Lisa and (me/I) _____ about the derailment.

42. The co-captains of the team are Julius and (him/he) _____.

43. She told me so (herself/themselves) _____.

44. I look like (her/she) _____.

45. (This is/These are) _____ the picture Degas painted.

46. Those keys are (mine/mines) _____.

47. She fixed the faucet without (anyone's/no one's) _____ help.

48. There was (a/this) _____ strange man waiting for the elevator.

49. Helen and (I/myself) _____ will be glad to help you.

50. Is this the tie (which/that) _____ you want to borrow?

51. The IRS sent a refund check to Dwight and (me/I) _____.

52. (Who's/Whose) _____ birthday are we celebrating?

53. He's the kind of person (who's/whose) _____ always patient.

54. To (us/we) _____, she always seemed young.

55. (Them/Those) _____ men are surveyors.

56. The police officer gave Pablo and (me/I) _____ the directions.

57. If there is anyone (who/whom) _____ disagrees, let him say so now.

58. He (himself/hisself) _____ didn't like the picture.

59. (Who/Whom) _____ do you think is telling the truth?

60. You don't know (anything/nothing) _____.

61. The man to (who/whom) _____ you have just spoken is my cousin.

62. She is the woman (who/whom) _____ owns twelve dogs.

63. (This here is/This here are/This is) _____ my nephew, John Bolger.

64. (Who/Whom) _____ does the director want to see?

65. We like to spoil (us/ourselves) _____.

66. They are the advisers (who/that) _____ are going to Lebanon.

67. The Mets, (who/whom) _____ won ten games straight, are in first place.

68. It must have been (them/they) _____ who rang the alarm.

69. You and (him/he) _____ are the instigators.

70. (That/Those) _____ isn't for sale.

Part C: In each sentence, use the appropriate form of the verb in parentheses.

71. I've _____ the same train all week. (take)

72. We had not _____ far when the tire blew. (go)

73. By the time Jim finishes reading his section of the paper, I will have _____ three. (read)

74. The ball was _____ by one of the outfielders. (catch)

75. By the end of the week, I will have _____ this gallon of ice cream. (eat)

76. That old trunk was _____ in the basement for years. (lie)

77. She has _____ another major in school. (choose)

78. The Hatfields and McCoys had _____ on the feud for many years. (carry)

79. Sonia was _____ for us at the station. (wait)

80. She is _____ her birthday cake. (cut)

81. They are _____ a well in their backyard. (dig)

82. We were _____ by mosquitoes on our camping trip. (bite)

Part D: Some of the following sentences are correct, but many have a verb form error. Underline any wrong form, and write the correct form in the blank.

_____ **83.** They have took a long time to answer my letter.

_____ **84.** We were'nt asked for our opinions.

_____ **85.** The river may have frozed already.

_____ **86.** I lended my car to my son.

_____ **87.** I move that the meeting is adjourned.

_____ 88. You have'nt forgotten what day it is, have you?

_____ 89. Elaine was gived a substantial raise by her manager.

_____ 90. The general demanded that he surrender.

_____ 91. Tina could have went already.

_____ 92. I knowed it was a bad idea.

_____ 93. The toddler has hid her shoes.

_____ 94. You could have stopped the argument.

_____ 95. We was robbed!

_____ 96. If I was he, I would learn how to drive.

Part E: Read each sentence below. If there is a mistake in the sentence, write the correction on the answer line. If there is no mistake, write "correct."

97. You're awful quiet today.

_____

98. The flowers smelled wonderfully.

_____

99. Jean seems the likeliest candidate for the office.

_____

100. He is the remarkablest man I've ever met.

_____

101. The magician appeared sudden.

_____

102. The suggestion was enthusiasticly endorsed by the committee.

_____

103. The news from the Middle East sounds badly.

_____

104. He didn't pass the driver's test as easily as he thought he would.

_____

105. Noisyly, the students entered the auditorium.

_____

106. This is the usefulest gadget we have.

_____

107. I don't feel very good; my stomach hurts.

_____

108. She's grown beautifuler over the years.

_____

109. They tasted the turtle soup tentative.

_____

110. His report was badder than I expected.

_____

111. Rats live longest than mice.

_____

112. The Bengals played terriblely this weekend.

_____

113. Berries taste most sweetest when they've been stored at room temperature for a few days.

_____

114. This room is more brighter with the new floor lamp.

_____

115. Sandra plays Chopin real beautifully.

_____

116. Between the two candidates, I like him best.

_____

117. He really behaved bad at the party.

_____

118. Sam was more cautious after he had made a few errors.

_____

119. Please make your recommendations specificer.

_____

120. Of all the managers in the factory, Charles is the more competent.

_____

121. He's insecurest when he's in a crowd.

_____

122. Alexis dresses most extravagantly than Liberace.

_____

123. Of the two quarterbacks, he's the least able passer.

_____

124. This recipe turned out more better than I thought it would.

_____

125. Of all the patients in the ward, she complained the less.

_____

In this chart, find the number of any item that you did not answer correctly. The right-hand side of the chart will tell you the pages to review if you missed more than one item in a given group.

If you missed item number	Review the following pages
1 2 3 4 5 6 7 8 9 10 11 12 13 14 15 16 17 18 19 20 21 22 23 24 25 26 27 28 29 30 31 32 33 34 35 36	Chapter 4, pages 52–60
37 38 39 40 41 42 43 44 45 46 47 48 49 50 51 52 53 54 55 56 57 58 59 60 61 62 63 64 65 66 67 68 69 70	Chapter 4, pages 55–56, 61–68
71 72 73 74 75 76 77 78 79 80 81 82	Chapter 4, pages 69–70

If you missed item number	Review the following pages
83 84 85 86 87 88 89 90 91 92 93 94 95 96	Chapter 4, pages 69–74 Chapter 6, pages 112–115
97 98 99 100 101 102 103 104 105 106 107 108 109 110 111 112 113 114 115 116 117 118 119 120 121 122 123 124 125	Chapter 4, pages 75–88

REVIEW TEST—CHAPTER 5. WORDS THAT GET SPECIAL TREATMENT

Part A: Rewrite each sentence using a contraction.

1. Do not tell anyone. _____

2. She is afraid. _____

3. They will be late. _____

4. I would like another glass of wine. _____

5. You have changed. _____

6. What is the matter with you? _____

7. He cannot make up his mind. _____

8. Dan has gone fishing. _____

9. There will not be enough volunteers. _____

10. You should not have come. _____

11. Mr. Garcia is retiring next month. _____

12. There has been an accident. _____

13. I have not received my mail. _____

14. There had been a fight earlier. _____

15. Who is on first? _____

16. I did not call him. _____

17. Somebody has taken my wallet! _____

18. How would you like your tea? _____

19. It will be dark soon. _____

20. Leslie has caught the virus. _____

Part B: In each sentence, choose the appropriate word in parentheses.

21. (Its/It's) _____ none of your business.

22. Jim and Arthur couldn't find (their/they're) _____ tickets.

23. I like a man (whose/who's) _____ well dressed.

24. (Your/You're) _____ walking out like that was very rude.

25. (There/They're) _____ a strange couple.

26. The grizzly bear was in (its/it's) _____ lair.

27. (Theirs/There's) _____ lipstick on your collar.

28. (Your/You're) _____ getting in my way.

29. She's a person (whose/who's) _____ judgment I value.

30. She's a person (whose/who's) _____ not easily discouraged.

31. That Mercedes is (theirs/there's) _____.

32. I enjoyed (your/you're) _____ singing.

33. (Whose/Who's) _____ eaten the last piece of pie?

34. Although (its/it's) _____ only early March, the trees are budding.

35. Tell me what (your/you're) _____ thinking.

36. (Its/It's) _____ teeth bared, the rabid dog approached me.

37. I wonder (whose/who's) _____ car that is.

38. Exercising when (your/you're) _____ tired is not fun.

39. (Their/They're) _____ greatest desire is to win the lottery.

40. He asked me (whose/who's) _____ paying for this.

Part C: In each sentence, choose the correct noun form.

41. The (managers/manager's/managers') _____ decision to change the pitcher came too late.

42. the (childrens/children's/childrens') _____ playground is well equipped.

43. His (daughters/daughter's/daughters') _____ birthdays all come in October.

44. It is (Grace and Marian/Grace's and Marian's/Grace and Marian's) _____ turn to provide refreshments for the meeting.

45. We are planning to take two (weeks/week's/weeks') _____ vacation.

46. The Queen of (Englands/England/England's) _____ jewels are priceless.

47. Cooking gourmet meals is (Karens/Karen's/Karens') _____ hobby.

48. The strike caused a (months/month's/months') _____ delay in deliveries.

49. The (butterflies/butterfly's/butterflies') have beautiful markings on their wings.

50. We toured (Jeffersons and Washingtons/Jefferson and Washington's/Jefferson's and Washington's) _____ homes.

51. Did you read the League of Women (Voters/Voter's/Voters') _____ pamphlet?

52. The (mens/men's/mens') _____ clothing department is on the second floor.

53. The (speakers/speaker's/speakers') _____ voices were difficult to hear.

54. I enjoy reading Robert (Frost/Frosts/Frost's) _____ poems.

55. The (directors/director's/directors') _____ of the project are studying the data.

56. (Someone/Someone's/Someones') _____ umbrella was left in the hall.

57. She bought ten (dollars/dollar's/dollars') _____ worth of gasoline.

58. She paid ten (dollars/dollar's/dollars') _____ for the gasoline.

59. Some (peoples/people's/peoples') _____ appetites are enormous.

60. The two (teams/team's/teams') _____ mascots taunted each other.

Part D: Assume that each of the following lines is a heading or title. Underline the first letter of every word that should be capitalized.

61. mom, the flag, and apple pie

62. daniel webster: a biography

63. the longest journey—my recovery from cancer

64. the war between the sexes

65. something to live for

66. america and russia: the cold war

67. moving on

68. love among the ruins

69. star trek—the movie

70. gone but not forgotten

Part E: In every sentence, underline the first letter of any word that should be capitalized.

71. is christmas on a wednesday this year?

72. dr. bradley is an english professor at the university of minnesota.

73. she selected a china pattern at the department store.

74. lincoln avenue is one block south of here.

75. the milky way is only one of perhaps billions of galaxies in the universe.

76. did you ever read *pride and prejudice*?

77. bishop desmond tutu, the general secretary of the south african council of churches, won the nobel peace prize in 1984.

78. i think reverend walker is a baptist minister.

79. the senators feared the spread of communism in central america.

80. my favorite time of the year is spring.

81. according to greek mythology, prometheus stole the gift of fire from the god zeus.

82. many people in the east practice hinduism.

83. pass the french fries, dad.

84. who is the presidential candidate for the democratic party?

85. titles of books, for example, *to kill a mockingbird,* are usually set in italics.

86. theodore roosevelt bolted the republican party in 1912 and ran on the progressive party ticket.

87. many christians were killed by the early roman emperors.

88. the city of pittsburgh was voted "most livable" this year.

89. tell us in your own words, lieutenant, what happened on the night of august 6, 1985.

90. mohammed had a revelation from allah, calling on him to reject paganism.

91. which is the closest planet to us?

92. my uncle was a sergeant in the war.

93. the eastern orthodox church observes easter next sunday, not today.

94. the year 622 is the beginning of the muslim lunar calendar.

95. many christian scientists refuse treatment by doctors.

96. our history class studied the rise of fascism in spain and italy before world war ii.

97. millions of jews were killed during the nazi regime.

98. how are you feeling today, grandfather?

99. the opera company is performing bizet's *carmen* during the fall season.

100. i think, doctor, that you'll be a fine professor.

In this chart, find the number of any item that you did not answer correctly. The right-hand side of the chart will tell you the pages to review if you missed more than one item in a given group.

If you missed item number	Review the following pages
1 2 3 4 5 6 7 8 9 10 11 12 13 14 15 16 17 18 19 20	Chapter 5, pages 89–92
21 22 23 24 25 26 27 28 29 30 31 32 33 34 35 36 37 38 39 40	Chapter 5, pages 92–93
41 42 43 44 45 46 47 48 49 50 51 52 53 54 55 56 57 58 59 60	Chapter 5, pages 94–97
61 62 63 64 65 66 67 68 69 70	Chapter 5, pages 97–99
71 72 73 74 76 77 78 79 80 81 82 83 84 85 86 87 88 89 90 91 92 93 94 95 96 97 98 99 100	Chapter 5, pages 100–109

POSTTEST

The following six-section test has been designed to help you assess which chapters of this book you need to re-study. Take as much time as you need to work through the entire test, and then check your answers. By filling out the chart at the end of the test, you will be able to identify which pages in this book you need to review.

Section 1

Part A: Underline the incorrect nouns in these sentences. Rewrite the words correctly in the answer blanks.

1. The news mediums reported on the crisises in Lebanon and Central America.

   _____

2. My grandmother wishes to catch some fishes.

   _____

3. *Geisha* are Japanese women trained since early childhood to be accomplished hostesses and entertainers.

   _____

4. Do you have any matchs to light these candles?

   _____

5. The two partys agreed on the criterions for the debate.

   _____

6. I like watching instant replaies during football games.

   _____

7. Some pharmacyes offer discounts to senior citizens on Wednesdays.

   _____

Part B: In each sentence, choose the correct noun form.

8. (Joes and Sams/Joe's and Sam's/Joe and Sam's) _____ deli is for sale.

9. All of the (childrens/children's/childrens') _____ art was displayed in the library.

10. Is the (city/city's/citys') _____ income tax form more complicated than the (state/state's/states') _____?

11. The jockey took us back to the (horses/horse's/horses')
    _____ stables.

12. Both the (lions and tigers/lions and tigers'/lions' and tigers')
    _____ cages were empty.

13. The *Pirates of Penzance* is one of (Gilbert and Sullivan/Gilbert's
    and Sullivan's/Gilbert and Sullivan's) _____ most
    popular operettas.

14. The (mans/men's/mens') _____ department is next to
    the young (boys/boy's/boys') _____ section.

Part C: Underline the first letter of any word that should be capitalized.

15. i'd like to introduce you to senator bert young.

16. many people like to do spring cleaning.

17. i enjoy doing the sunday crossword puzzle in *the new york times*.

18. i hope you're feeling better, grandma.

19. the mayors held a news conference at the fairmont hotel.

20. none of the street signs in the city were printed in arabic numerals.

21. in early christianity, the followers of christ were sometimes called
    "nazarenes."

22. some of the doctors refused to cross the technicians' picket line.

23. the democratic party held its convention in san francisco.

24. i mailed the letter to my state senator in a manila envelope.

25. the british colonies on this continent attracted many protestant sects
    seeking religious freedom.

26. i think christmas is my favorite time of the year.

27. will professor wilkins be giving us a mid-term exam?

28. do you plan on giving us a mid-term exam, professor?

29. the roots of democracy are found in the history of ancient greece.

30. many hindus believe in reincarnation.

31. texas is often referred to as the lone star state.

32. the boy scouts of america was founded in 1910.

33. in 1929, thomas wolfe published *look homeward, angel.*

34. we traded in our chevrolet for a new toyota.

35. in some european democracies, the communist party is quite popular.

Section 2

Part A: In each sentence, use the appropriate form of the verb in parentheses.

1. She has _____ distant over the past few months. (become)

2. Andy was _____ to have a bad temper. (know)

3. By the time we get there, they will have _____. (eat)

4. At the entrance of the cave, they had _____ down to rest. (lie)

5. You were _____ the same sweater when I saw you last. (knit)

6. Have you _____ my secret? (keep)

7. I was _____ a shower when the phone rang. (take)

8. Many Indian tribes were _____ from their lands by the settlers. (drive)

9. He had _____ that picture of me in his wallet for years. (carry)

10. The oak tree's leaves are _____ earlier this year. (drop)

11. They will have _____ by now. (leave)

12. The conductor is furiously _____ out the rhythm to the band. (beat)

Part B: Underline any incorrect verb form, and write the correct form in the blank. If a sentence contains no error, write "correct" in the blank.

_____ 13. She's began to recover from the shock.

_____ 14. You've bit off more than you can chew.

_____ 15. My wife may have spoke to you already about our plans.

_____ 16. In 1915 the *Lusitania* was sank by a German submarine.

_____ 17. This exercise is'nt very difficult.

_____ 18. The wind blowed down the power lines along the boulevard.

_____ 19. If Benjamin Franklin was alive today, he'd be amazed by the latest technology.

_____ 20. *Invisible Man* was wrote by Ralph Ellison.

_____ 21. I digged a hole in the backyard and planted the azalea bush.

_____ 22. The Fosters have been having some trouble with termites.

_____ 23. The men in the overturned sailboat couldn't have swam ashore.

_____ 24. The maitre d' insisted that he leaves at once.

_____ 25. "I would'nt want to intrude," I said politely.

_____ 26. If I were president, I'd negotiate at this time.

Section 3

Choose the correct verb form in each sentence.

1. There (is/are) _____ a begonia and a spider plant in the window.

2. (Do/Does) _____ each of these parrots talk?

3. They (was/were) _____ not willing to do all that extra work.

4. My parents' car (has/have) _____ a flat tire.

5. My relatives in Italy (visit/visits) _____ us every two years.

6. Many (was/were) _____ overcome by the toxic fumes.

7. Alice and Ted (don't/doesn't) _____ live here anymore.

8. She or her sister (has/have) _____ consulted a lawyer.

9. The thing I hated most (was/were) _____ the boring speeches.

10. (Don't/Doesn't) _____ anyone here have any manners?

11. What kinds of food (do/does) _____ a guinea pig eat?

12. (Isn't/Aren't) _____ the price of the repairs a little steep?

13. The family (do/does) _____ not want to move.

14. Everyone (take/takes) _____ a coffee break in the morning.

15. The pyramids of Egypt (has/have) _____ withstood the ravages of the desert for many centuries.

16. Jazz and country (is/are) _____ my favorite types of music.

17. Some parts of the test (has/have) _____ tricky questions.

18. All last summer, the mosquitos (was/were) _____ a terrible problem.

19. Chess as well as checkers (is/are) _____ played on this board.

20. The wine in these bottles (taste/tastes) _____ sour.

21. Most of it (don't/doesn't) _____ make any sense.

22. Few (disagree/disagrees) _____ with his assessment of the situation.

23. Where in the medicine chest (is/are) _____ the cold tablets kept?

24. Over one-fourth of the people on earth (is/are) _____ Chinese.

25. Here (come/comes) _____ the man we all admire.

26. Several of the people in the audience (was/were) _____ booing.

27. The crew (is/are) _____ from six different countries.

28. Neither of the contenders (is/are) _____ really a good fighter.

29. The wife and child of the trapped man (wait/waits) _____ anxiously near the mine entrance.

30. Two-thirds of the community fund (has/have) _____ been distributed.

31. Half of the funds (was/were) _____ stolen.

32. The orchestra (play/plays) _____ music by Sousa every Fourth of July.

33. Neither of those pens (work/works) _____ very well.

34. (Is/Are) _____ mathematics or economics your major?

35. Something (seem/seems) _____ to be troubling you.

36. Coffee and a roll (is/are) _____ known as a "continental breakfast."

37. One of the doctors (don't/doesn't) _____ practice medicine anymore.

38. Either Miami or San Francisco (is/are) _____ a good bet to win the Super Bowl.

39. The captain, accompanied by his chief assistant, (inspect/inspects) _____ the platoon.

40. (Has/Have) _____ the jury returned a verdict?

Section 4

In each sentence, choose the correct pronoun form.

1. Janet and (me/I) _____ went shopping for new bathing suits.

2. Were Barry and (him/he) _____ roommates in college?

3. The police officer gave Michael and (we/us) _____ a lecture on using seatbelts.

4. She wished Susan and (me/I) _____ good luck.

5. I have ordered tickets for you and (me/I) _____.

6. Below (us/we) _____ crashed the waves.

7. It was (me/I) _____ whom they called.

8. Could it have been (her/she) _____ who left the message?

9. You were as efficient as (him/he) _____.

10. Their children don't look at all like (them/they) _____.

11. Roger and (I/myself) _____ are planning a trip to Haiti.

12. Did we give (us/ourselves) _____ enough time to get there?

13. They liked my friend and (me/myself) _____.

14. The twins (theirselves/themselves) _____ can't tell each other apart.

15. He (hisself/himself) _____ said it wouldn't work.

16. (There/Their/They're) _____ clothing was worn and patched.

17. That's not yours, that's (mine/mines) _____.

18. Those seats are (our's/ours) _____.

19. (Theirs/There's) _____ no business like show business.

20. (There/Their/They're) _____ constant bickering affected the children.

21. The guard dog only responds to (its/it's) _____ master.

22. (Your/You're) _____ singing was scaring the dog.

23. I don't trust (those/them) _____ politicians.

24. (Is this/Are these) _____ your glasses?

25. (That is/Those are) _____ my neighbors' cat.

26. (This here/This) _____ is my great-uncle, Oscar.

27. I met (this/a) _____ guy on the street the other day.

28. Tom is one of those men (who/that) _____ is always late.

29. The car, (which/that) _____ is a two-door compact, will be ready to be picked up on Monday.

30. (Whose/Who's) _____ idea was this, anyway?

31. The man, with (who/whom) _____ I was just speaking, say he knows you.

32. (Who/Whom) _____ do you think will win the election?

33. Wasn't it Marie Curie (who/whom) _____ discovered the properties of radium?

34. Mark, (who/whom) _____ everyone calls "Bucky," hates nicknames.

35. (Who/Whom) _____ did they elect?

36. I wonder (who/whom) _____ she's dating now.

37. I never told (anyone/no one) _____ about your plastic surgery.

38. Is there (anyone/somebody) _____ here who can help me?

Section 5

Part A: Choose the correct article, adjective, or adverb form in each of these sentences.

1. Many women at the turn of the century wanted (a/an) _____ hourglass figure.

2. They're planning (a/an) _____ European vacation.

3. This is (a/an) _____ historic moment.

4. He (subtlely/subtly) _____ asked me to stop snoring.

5. The safe opened (automatically/automaticly) _____.

6. The chairman (hastyly/hastily) _____ called for a vote by the board.

7. That bus driver is (incompetent/incompetently) _____.

8. They were (real/really) _____ glad to see us.

9. They tasted the stew (suspicious/suspiciously) _____.

10. Those cheerleaders are very (enthusiastic/enthusiastically) _____.

11. The traffic is moving (awful/awfully) _____ slowly this morning.

12. He always appears (happy/happily) _____.

13. The amateurs acted (horrible/horribly) _____ in that play.

14. Without a sound, the caped crusader appeared (sudden/suddenly) _____.

Part B: Find the comparison mistakes in these sentences. Rewrite the sentences correctly. There is one correct sentence.

15. This is the excitingest hockey game of the season.

_____

16. Of the two centers, Malone was tallest.

_____

17. He's willinger than I am to accept their explanation.

_____

18. Of the two, Jim, read the directions most carefully.

_____

19. The landlord made the repairs quicklyer than usual.

_____

20. This is the worse coffee I've ever had.

_____

21. In general, elephants live longest than monkeys.

_____

22. You smiled brightliest of all.

_____

23. Of the three dancers, she was the less graceful.

_____

24. Watergate was one of the most shamefulest incidents in U.S. history.

_____

25. The first debater spoke more passionatelier than all the others.

_____

26. Tony felt well again after his stay in the hospital.

_____

27. Hayes plays bass guitar good.

_____

28. Sampson leaps more higher than Erving.

_____

29. After talking to a psychologist, she appeared least nervous.

_____

30. Hernandez was voted the more valuable player on the team.

_____

31. Signals from the repaired satellite were coming back more clearlyer.

_____

32. This movie is funniest than the one we saw last night.

_____

33. Your handwriting is worst than mine.

_____

34. The team really played bad today.

_____

Section 6

Part A: Some of the sentences below are complete, some are incomplete. Rewrite a complete sentence using capital letter(s) and the correct end punctuation. If the sentence is not complete, write "incomplete sentence" in the blank.

1. later we heard that our team had won easily

_____

2. after a long absence

   _____

3. have you heard the rumor yet

   _____

4. outside the stadium

   _____

5. the skipper cast off the lines

   _____

6. pass the mustard

   _____

7. unless you pay me soon

   _____

8. hooray i won the lottery

   _____

9. he asked if i wanted a lift

   _____

10. why don't you wait for me in the lobby

    _____

Part B: Assume that each of the following lines is a heading or title. Underline the first letter of every word that should be capitalized.

11. catch me if you can
12. someone to talk to
13. wrestling—the story of the squared circle
14. nixon: an autobiography
15. dancing among the daisies

In this chart, find the number of any item that you did not answer correctly. The right-hand side of the chart will tell you the pages to review if you missed more than one item in a given group.

If you missed item number	Review the following pages
Section 1 1 2 3 4 5 6 7	Chapter 1, page 2; Chapter 6, pages 110–111
8 9 10 11 12 13 14	Chapter 5, pages 94–96
15 16 17 18 19 20 21 22 23 24 25 26 27 28 29 30 31 32 33 34 35	Chapter 1, pages 1–3; Chapter 5, pages 100–109
Section 2 1 2 3 4 5 6 7 8 9 10 11 12	Chapter 1, pages 6–13; Chapter 4, pages 69–70; Chapter 6, pages 112–115
13 14 15 16 17 18 19 20 21 22 23 24 25 26	Chapter 1, pages 6–12; Chapter 4, pages 69–74; Chapter 5, pages 89–91
Section 3 1 2 3 4 5 6 7 8 9 10 11 12 13 14 15 16 17 18 19 20 21 22 23 24 25 26 27 28 29 30 31 32 33 34 35 36 37 38 39 40	Chapter 2, pages 32–38; Chapter 3, pages 49–50; Chapter 4, pages 52–60
Section 4 1 2 3 4 5 6 7 8 9 10 11 12 13 14 15 16 17 18 19 20 21 22 23 24 25 26 27 28 29 30 31 32 33 34 35 36 37 38	Chapter 1, pages 21–26; Chapter 2, pages 38–43; Chapter 4, pages 61–67 & 84; Chapter 5, pages 92–93

If you missed item number	Review the following pages
Section 5 1 2 3 4 5 6 7 8 9 10 11 12 13 14 15 16 17 18 19 20 21 22 23 24 25 26 27 28 29 30 31 32 33 34	Chapter 1, pages 14–21; Chapter 2, pages 44–45; Chapter 4, pages 85–88 Chapter 4, pages 75–83
Section 6 1 2 3 4 5 6 7 8 9 10	Chapter 3, pages 46–51
11 12 13 14 15	Chapter 5, pages 97–99

INDEX